# STENCILING TECHNIQUES

# STENCILING TECHNIQUES

## A COMPLETE GUIDE TO TRADITIONAL AND CONTEMPORARY DESIGNS FOR THE HOME

## JANE GAUSS

WITH THE ARTISTS AND DESIGNERS OF
THE STENCIL ARTISANS LEAGUE, INC.

WATSON-GUPTILL PUBLICATIONS/NEW YORK

DEDICATION

This book is dedicated with love to Adele Bishop—an artist of genuine beauty, grace, warmth, and style. Adele first introduced me to professional stenciling at a three-day seminar where I learned how to develop my passion for stenciling into a full-time career. She subsequently became my mentor and teacher during a two-year Master Teacher training program. When I began to teach national seminars, I saw firsthand how her techniques and creativity affected so many lives.

In 1986, Adele graciously accepted my request to be SALI's guest of honor at our first national convention in Arlington, Virginia. She offered the assembly encouraging words, expressing her pride in the direction the League had chosen to pursue and challenging us never to lose sight of excellence earned through hard work, education, and dedication. Her influence and support have helped SALI become the internationally recognized decorative arts organization that it is today.

Senior Editor: Candace Raney
Edited by Joy Aquilino
Designed by Areta Buk
Graphic production by Hector Campbell

Photo on page 1: Quilts designed and stenciled by Judith Barker and Julia Hierl Burmesch for American Traditional.
Photo on pages 2–3: Designed by Jane Gauss for Plaid Enterprises. From *The Complete Book of Wall Stenciling* by Jane Gauss, copyright © 1984 by Plaid Enterprises. Courtesy of Plaid Enterprises, Inc.

The images as noted on pages 2–3, 11, 24–25, 46, 47, 49, 51, and 70–71 copyright © by Plaid Enterprises, Inc., P.O. Box 760, Norcross, Georgia 30091-7600. Used with express permission. All rights reserved. Plaid Enterprises manufactures a complete line of stencils, stencil paints, and instructional books under the brand name STENCIL DECOR®.

On page 63: The lattice wall border by Sandra Buckingham originally appeared in *Stencilling: A Harrowsmith Guide* by Sandra Buckingham (North York, Ontario, and Buffalo, New York: Camden House Publishing, 1989).

Copyright © 1995 by Jane Gauss

First published in 1995 by Watson-Guptill Publications, a division of BPI Communications, Inc., 1515 Broadway, New York, N.Y. 10036

**Library of Congress Cataloging-in-Publication Data**
Gauss, Jane.
    Stenciling techniques: a complete guide to traditional and contemporary designs for the home / Jane Gauss.
        p.    cm.
    Includes bibliographical references and index.
    ISBN 0-8230-4992-2
    1. Stencil work—Amateurs' manuals.    2. Interior decoration—Amateurs' manuals.    I. Title.
TT270.G38 1995
745.7'3—dc20                                            95-24583
                                                            CIP

Manufactured in Hong Kong

First printing, 1995

3  4  5  6  7  8  9 / 03  02  01  00  99

# PREFACE

My reasons for writing *Stenciling Techniques: A Complete Guide to Traditional and Contemporary Designs for the Home* are very simple: To share the joy that stenciling has brought me, and to proclaim the successes of the many gifted stencilers of the Stencil Artisans League, Inc.

What you learn from this book will be determined by your stenciling skills and experience. Regardless of your level of expertise, *Stenciling Techniques* will inspire you and challenge you to grow creatively. For the first-time stenciler, it's a complete how-to guide. For someone who has dabbled in stenciling but isn't sure they want to pursue it wholeheartedly, this book is a testament to the benefits of learning more about stenciling and developing a personal style. For the professional designer, stenciler, and decorative painter, it serves as a reference for prospective clients, presenting a multitude of designs, styles, and surfaces that lend themselves to stenciling. Through the work of its contributors, this book proves without a doubt that there's more than one way to stencil. The techniques shown herein can serve as a starting point or can be incorporated into your own style.

Above all, I've written *Stenciling Techniques* so that you could experience the same delight in stenciling that each SALI member experiences and shares. Our talents are God's gift to each of us, and what we do with those talents and the ways in which we touch others' lives are our gifts to God. I hope that you'll share what you learn from this book by expressing your own personal style through stenciling.

## ACKNOWLEDGMENTS

*Stenciling Techniques* would not exist without the contributions of the many gifted artists and designers of the Stencil Artisans League. I am indebted to the members of the League for their contributions and support, and hope that this book will be the first of many to celebrate stenciling and those who strive to maintain the standards of excellence that we all enjoy today.

A special thank you to the members of my staff at Stenciler's Emporium, who sandwiched in the tasks that helped create this book, and especially for shouldering the additional weight of my responsibilities so that I could spend time away from the office. Special thanks to Claire Andorka, an English major at Hiram College, for her very meticulous assistance at the computer; to Nancy Forester, who helped with the photography and managed the office so that I could have time away to write; and to Joy Aquilino for her editing, and the final push to make all of this come together.

# CONTENTS

# INTRODUCTION

## WHAT IS STENCILING?

Stenciling is the process of applying paint or powdered pigment into the cut-out areas of a material that is impervious to paint. It has been identified as the most primitive form of printing, and as such has been used by cultures dating back to the ancient Egyptians (around 2500 B.C.) Like so many art forms, stenciling seems to have appeared without a distinct point of origin. It was often used as a means to print or decorate a variety of surfaces, and then abandoned as other techniques were developed. Cloth, heavy paper, waxed papers, and even delicately woven human hairs were used as the first stencils.

The word "stenciling" evolved during the Middle Ages in France, from the French *estenceler* ("to sparkle") and the Latin *scintilla* ("to spark"). It was the French who first used stencils to add glistening decorations to their wallpapers, books, fabrics, and playing cards. In Europe during the late 16th and 17th centuries, stenciling appeared in the homes of the wealthy. It was at this time that Europeans first began to migrate to America. These settlers longed for the color and ornamentation of their native lands, yet their poverty and struggle for freedom prevented most of them from decorating their homes beyond the barest essentials.

## EARLY AMERICAN STENCILING STYLES

The period of stenciling that has been revived in so many of today's country decorating themes is that of the itinerant artists of New England, who were active from 1760 to 1840, when stenciling and mural painting were fashionable in the wealthy homes of the east. Scenic wallpapers imported from Europe were expensive, and depicted distant scenes such as Grecian gardens or palatial European estates, or famous battles fought on the Continent. Stenciling and mural painting provided well-to-do homeowners with some individuality of expression, inspiring itinerant artists to paint and stencil the local countryside and its flora and fauna. These charming motifs and images were influenced by several European models, including German, Dutch, English, and French designs. In general, each wall was treated as a separate space and motifs were applied by eye rather than by careful measurement. In addition to walls and floors, decorative painting from this period was applied to a wide range of surfaces, including fireplace surrounds, mantles, fireboards, boxes, and canvas floorcloths.

Historians have traced surviving stencil designs to approximately fifteen itinerant artists. Many of these designs have been attributed to Moses Eaton, Jr., who worked and traveled in New England circa 1800 to 1840. Eaton's bright patterns on warm backgrounds suggest an industrious home life spent close to the hearth and a profound appreciation of nature. Their simplicity and boldness lend an atmosphere of gaiety and informality to any setting. Another well-known itinerant artist is Rufus Porter, an associate of Eaton's who specialized in freehand paintings and murals. His style is currently enjoying a revival, as contemporary trompe l'oeil artists create wall murals based on his designs. (See also "Stenciled Floors," pages 68–69.)

Unfortunately, much of the stenciling from this period has been lost, as homes were remodeled, torn down, or destroyed by time and neglect. Thanks to Janet Waring, who began her research in 1924, there is an extensive record of the decorative art of that era. She traveled throughout New England, tracing stencil patterns that adorned walls, floors, and furniture. While visiting the Eaton family homestead, she discovered Moses Eaton's stencil box in the attic. The seventy-eight stencils she found comprised approximately forty complete designs. There were no registration marks on these stencils, as Eaton had a keen eye for placement as well as for color and design relationships.

Janet Waring's book, *Early American Wall Stencils,* was first published in 1937. (The revised edition is currently available in libraries and bookstores.) The stencil designs of the itinerant artists are also available in several copyright-free collections, for you to enlarge, embellish, and use in your own home. You can also contact Polly Forcier, owner of MB Historic Decor (see page 136 for more information), who carries an extensive assortment of precut historic stencils for borders, full wall treatments, and floors.

## ADELE BISHOP AND THE STENCILING RENAISSANCE OF THE 1970s

For a number of reasons, including the influence of Modernism on American art and design, decorative painting fell out of fashion in the mid-20th century. As a result of the American bicentennial in 1976 and the innovative efforts of Adele Bishop and her partner Cile Lord in the decade preceding it, interest in an American decorative heritage was renewed. Bishop unexpectedly came across *Early American Wall Stencils* in the late 1950s, and was so impressed with the simplicity and dignity of the stencil designs that she decided to try to recreate them in her own home.

Although Adele had never stenciled before, it occurred to her that a transparent stencil material would enable her to trace directly from patterns more accurately, and to create a logical system of register marks for overlays and repeats. She first used acetate book covers for this purpose, since at the time the only material used to make stencils was an opaque manila board. She had also read about a product used primarily by the sign-painting trade called "japan paint," which dried instantly and could be used on hard surfaces. With French handmade brushes, which she used to apply paint in a circular motion, she was able to duplicate the soft, translucent look of the early American designs.

## HISTORIC STENCIL PATTERNS

These patterns, which were adapted from *Early American Design Motifs* (edited by Suzanne E. Chapman; Dover Publications: 1974), represent the range of design and complexity of the stencil motifs of late-18th and early-19th century America.

*Wall stencils from the Josiah Sage house in South Sandisfield, Massachusetts.*

*Wall stencil and pineapple motif by Moses Eaton, from the Grant house in North Saco, Maine.*

*Wall stencil from the Jesse Ayer house in Hampstead, New Hampshire.*

*Wall stencil from the Mansel Alcock house in Hancock, New Hampshire.*

Encouraged by the success she enjoyed with these innovations, Adele brought her work to the attention of the decorating establishment. Unfortunately, the early American decorative style wasn't widely recognized until the mid-1970s. Undeterred by her lukewarm reception, Adele turned her energies toward creating a broader and more sophisticated approach to decorative design. She realized that transparent materials could be used to produce practically any design in stencil form, and that a design's complexity was no longer an obstacle, as she could use as many overlays as were necessary to recreate it.

In the early 1960s, Adele taught Cile Lord, a friend and fine artist, how to stencil. Soon thereafter they founded Bishop & Lord, a custom stenciling business located in New York City. Using Bishop's materials and application methods and inspired by sources as wide-ranging as ancient civilizations and abstract art, they made remarkable advancements in decoration and design and received many favorable reviews. Eventually, the attention generated by the media created a seemingly insurmountable problem for others who wanted to stencil: the scarcity of stencils and stenciling materials. In 1968, Bishop & Lord produced a stencil kit containing die-cut stencils, paints, brushes, and an illustrated instruction book, which they sold through a small mail order business in Vermont called American Decorative Arts, Inc.

Bishop & Lord was dissolved in 1970, when Adele moved to Vermont to expand her mail order business and Cile continued working as a custom stenciler in New York. In 1972, Adele and Cile were asked by Viking-Penguin to write and illustrate a definitive book on stenciling. Their book, *The Art of Decorative Stenciling,* was published in 1976 to coincide with the American bicentennial. Although the publication, national promotion, and distribution of the book was successful, the stenciling materials used by Cile and Adele were still somewhat difficult to obtain, as Adele's mail order business was their only source. At that point, stenciling had still not been recognized as a craft by any national craft, art supply, or decorating company.

In spite of this, interest in stenciling continued to increase. Assisted by her colleagues Kathie Marron-Wall and Zilda McKinstry, Adele responded by developing a three-day stenciling seminar. In addition to acquiring proficiency in stenciling, students were instructed in effective teaching methods, careers in custom stenciling, historic restoration, producing craft items for sale, and starting their own businesses. In 1982, Adele began publishing a quarterly newsletter, *The Stenciler's Guild News Letter,* which provided seminar graduates with up-to-date information about the decorative stenciling community.

It is through Adele's influence and persistence that so many stencilers were made aware of this important craft, and were able to use their love of color and decorating to start their own businesses. Today stenciling is experiencing a second renaissance, not only in the Americas, but in Europe and Asia as well.

*Detail from a stenciled wall mural based on the style of Rufus Porter, an itinerant artist active during the early 19th century. This particular example was done in a monochromatic color scheme to fit a client's needs. Designed and stenciled by Linda Carter Lefko.*

*The stencil motifs of the wall and chest (left) and canvas floorcloth (right) are based on early American designs. The motif on the chest is adapted from a traditional quilt block. Wall and chest designed and stenciled by Adele Bishop and Cile Lord; floorcloth designed and stenciled by Adele Bishop.*

*A restored Victorian oak mantle and woodwork provide the perfect framework for an assortment of primitive-style stencil motifs. Designed and stenciled by Anita Alsup.*

*Historic designs were adapted for this 20th-century rustic kitchen. Designed and stenciled by Jane Gauss for Plaid Enterprises. From* The Complete Book of Wall Stenciling *by Jane Gauss, copyright © 1984 by Plaid Enterprises. Courtesy of Plaid Enterprises, Inc.*

## STENCILING STYLE TODAY

As we trace the thread of stenciling through history, it becomes apparent that it has helped satisfy the inherent human need to modify and personalize interiors. This form of cultural communication reflects lifestyle, personality, and economic status. As the 21st century approaches, we can be certain that stenciling will affect posterity in the same way.

During the last quarter of the 20th century, we have seen a renewed awareness and interest in the decorative past, as well as an attempt to integrate elements of that heritage into our homes. This spawned the eclectic style of decorating, in which a mixture of styles and objects, both old and new, are integrated to produce a unique decor—a perfect environment for stenciling!

As a decorating medium, stenciling is as stable as paint and wallpaper, and will remain a practical and desirable decorating trend regardless of current fads. In fact, as decorating trends peak, they are often imitated by the wallpaper industry. For instance, wallpapers that mimicked primitive stenciling flooded the market in the 1980s. In the 1990s, the trend has shifted to wallpapers that simulate faux finishes such as marbling, rag-rolling, and sponging, and feature freeform patterns that accent architectural elements. Shown below and opposite are but a few examples of the latest trends in stenciling and decorative painting.

Another very strong influence on the future of stenciling is the Stencil Artisan League, Inc. (SALI). Founded in 1984, this organization is dedicated to perpetuating some of the oldest art forms known to the human race: stenciling, faux finishing, and related decorative arts. This book is a testament to the work of SALI and the members who have been instrumental in the growth of this very prestigious organization during its first decade. For information on how to contact SALI, see page 136.

*Block printing's loose, flowing designs complement a range of surfaces and interior decors. The lightly textured walls of this living room are elegantly enhanced by a block-printed iris garden. (See "Block Printing," page 39.) Designed and block-printed by Vi and Stu Cutbill.*

The textured plaster walls and ceiling of a small sunroom are a perfect venue for this "wish upon a star" motif, in which the Man in the Moon is harassed by a menacing cherub. The ceiling was sponged with several colors of interior latex flat wall paint, from light yellow (to provide a background glow for the night sky) to a combination of purple, white, and navy that was gradually lightened as the sky flowed onto the wall. The completed sky was then sprinkled with gold leaf stars. (See also "Stenciled Interiors," pages 44–69, and "Stenciling a Ceiling," page 60.) Stencils from L 'n J Designs; stenciled by Linda Nelson Johnson and Lori Rohde.

Bring your garden indoors—transform an interior space with stenciling. Create a three-dimensional effect by using several values of one color within each motif and by adding shadows to suggest pictorial depth. (See also "Advanced Techniques," pages 104–123.) Designed and stenciled by Susan Kolb.

You can stencil a wide range of surfaces, including fabrics, wood, and ceramic tile. Here, a plain white apron is embellished with an ivy and ribbon stencil. (See also "Other Stenciling Projects," pages 70–103, and "Fabrics," page 78. This pattern, which was also used on the tile rug on page 90, appears on pages 130–134.) Designed and stenciled by Jane Gauss.

*The primitive-style motifs in this sunny parlor were stenciled with japan paints, handmade artist's brushes, and stencils cut from clear acetate. Adele Bishop was among the first to use transparent materials and japan paints for stenciling. Stencil designs from* Early American Wall Stencils *by Janet Waring, published in 1937. Designed and stenciled by Adele Bishop.*

# MATERIALS AND TOOLS

The recent surge of interest in stenciling has produced a virtual flood of products and designs, a constantly expanding selection of types, colors, and exciting innovations for home decorating. This sudden growth in the number and variety of stenciling products has in turn increased quality and lowered prices, as manufacturers and stencil designers compete for their fair share of the market. In an attempt to attract the hesitant beginner, more products designed for the first-time stenciler are being offered than ever before.

This chapter reviews stenciling's three fundamental material requirements—a template through which paint is applied, the paint itself, and an applicator—and explains the benefits and drawbacks of working with the various products in each category. The steps involved in designing and cutting your own stencils are also outlined, with tips on adapting stencil patterns from motifs in your decor.

# STENCILING SUPPLIES

One of stenciling's most inviting attributes is its versatility—there are no "right" or "wrong" materials, or even hard-and-fast rules for using them. As you experiment with the materials discussed in this chapter, and as your stenciling skills (and comfort level) improve, you will develop preferences for certain products and your own ways of using them. If you discover an item or devise an approach that helps you achieve a particular look, as long as it doesn't impede your project's progress—or dampen your enthusiasm for it—you can consider yourself a stenciling innovator.

As you study this book for instruction and inspiration, carefully read through each project description to see which materials were used and how the stenciler applied them. This will give you an idea of the kinds of products you will need to stencil your particular project, surface, and decor.

## PRECUT STENCILS

Before the stenciling renaissance of the mid-1970s, the availability of high-quality precut stencils was extremely limited. As a result, many stencilers were obliged to design and cut their own stencils, either by adapting historic designs or creating their own. Today there are literally thousands of precut stencils available in a wide range of styles, with new designs appearing each month. Precut stencils are particularly useful to beginners, for whom simply tracing and cutting a stencil pattern can be intimidating, and who instead should focus on learning to work with paint. Once you've mastered the basic procedures for applying paint outlined in the next chapter, you can try your hand at creating an original stencil. (See "Designing and Cutting Your Own Stencils," pages 20–22.)

Every stencil has two components: *windows,* which are the openings through which paint is applied; and *bridges,* which are the parts of the stencil that separate the openings. Precut stencils are made from a variety of materials, both opaque (treated cardboard, heavy paper, and metal) and transparent (polyester film, acetate, and Mylar). When working with *multi-overlay stencils*—those whose motifs are divided among several stencils to allow for the precise

*Precut stencils are made from a variety of materials, including cardboard, metal, and polyester film.*

coloring of specific areas or because their motifs are too close together to permit adequate bridges—transparent materials make it easier to accurately line up the elements of a design. Consistently durable and flexible materials and computerized laser cutting make today's precut stencils accurate and easy to use.

## STENCILING PAINTS

In many ways, paint is the most critical component of a stenciling project. Many kinds of paints are suitable for stenciling; in fact, you can use practically any paint. Before making a choice, however, you must determine which paint will produce the look you want on the surface you'll be stenciling and has a consistency that you can manage comfortably, as paint with a runny or watery consistency is very difficult to control. Keep in mind that the most desirable paints are quick-drying, so that stencils can be repositioned almost instantly. You should also consider the following:

- What are the *physical characteristics of the surface* you'll be stenciling (glossy or matte, smooth or rough)?
- What sort of *surface preparation* is required? The answer to this question varies from project to project. For instance, a wall or ceiling will require a washing or a fresh coat of paint; a piece of prefinished furniture will need sanding or stripping; and fabrics may require laundering and ironing. Before you begin your stenciling project, make sure you've taken the proper steps to ensure its durability.
- What about *day-to-day use?* Will the stenciling be in a high-traffic area or on an item that needs frequent washing, or, if outdoors, some kind of exterior surface protection?
- What about *cleanup?* Some paints clean up almost effortlessly, whereas others require solvents and/or the immediate and thorough cleaning of stencils, brushes, and other applicators.
- *How much paint* is needed? In general, a little paint goes a long way in stenciling. For example, one 2-ounce container of acrylic or japan paint or one stencil crayon or container of stencil cream provides adequate coverage for moderately complex borders in two to three average-sized rooms. You should take into account whether your finish will be opaque or transparent; depending on the type of paint, the former might require more than one application.

The following is an overview of the types of paints that are formulated expressly for stenciling. Consider the advantages and disadvantages of each and review the application techniques outlined in the next chapter (see pages 23–31) before making your first purchase.

### ACRYLIC PAINTS
Acrylic paints, which are water-based, are available in two forms: *fluid acrylics,* which are packaged in 2-ounce plastic squeeze bottles, and *tube acrylics,* which are often used by

fine artists. Fluid acrylics come in a wide range of colors and dry very quickly, while tube acrylics are available in fewer colors, are more expensive than fluid acrylics, and generally require slightly longer drying times than fluid acrylics because they are more heavily pigmented. Tube acrylics appeal to the fine-artist-turned-stenciler who prefers to custom-mix colors on a palette.

Acrylics dry quickly to an opaque, satiny, durable finish that is impervious to water. Moreover, acrylics will begin to thicken and cure when exposed to the air. This characteristic requires the use of an extender or other solvent such as isopropyl rubbing alcohol to maintain paint consistency and to keep paint from drying on brushes or stencils (see page 26). It also means that you must be scrupulous about cleaning your brushes and stencils after you finish stenciling for the day. You can use either one of the commercial brush cleaners expressly formulated for acrylic paints, or a household cleaning soap like Murphy's Oil Soap and warm water.

Once you've gained some practice working with acrylics straight out of the bottle and you'd like to make softer, more translucent prints, you can try adding *acrylic gel medium* to your paint. This increases the paint's "open" time without altering its consistency and enhances its luminosity and transparency, making lustrous glazes of color possible.

Acrylics can be used on virtually any surface that can be painted, as long as it doesn't have a high sheen. An additive known as *textile medium* can be mixed with acrylic paint to produce a colorfast stencil print on fabric. This product breaks down the acrylic binder, allowing the pigments to bond with the fabric and softening the paint film so that it's more flexible after it dries. (See also "Fabric Paints," below.)

### JAPAN PAINTS

Japan paints are oil-based paints that contain a quick-drying additive. Formulated for use on hard surfaces and originally used by sign painters, these paints were first used for stenciling in the late 1950s by Adele Bishop, who wanted the richness and translucency of traditional tube oil paints but without the long drying times they require. In fact, even after acrylics were adopted by the stenciling community, many professional stencilers continued to favor japan paints for their soft, transparent prints and smooth consistency of application. Japan paints do have a few drawbacks, however: They are not as easily obtainable as acrylics, their limited palette requires that many colors be mixed, and they must be thinned and cleaned up with solvents such as turpentine and mineral spirits. The potential health hazards of these solvents have motivated many stencilers to switch to watersoluble acrylic or solid stenciling paints.

Japan paints do not bond well to glossy surfaces, including walls with a semi-gloss finish. As they cannot be set with heat, japan paints should not be used on fabrics.

### STENCIL CRAYONS AND CREAMS

The solid or so-called "dry" paints are the latest advance in stenciling materials. Available in sticks or crayons and in small plastic or glass jars, these paints were initially oil-based. Some brands are now watersoluble, requiring only soap and water or a watersoluble brush cleaner for clean up. Solid stencil paints have revolutionized stenciling, particularly for beginners, by essentially eliminating the common problem of applying too much paint with too much pressure, which results in a wet, smudged print. The colors blend beautifully and can be used to create both opaque and transparent looks, with little paint buildup on stencils or brushes.

Stencil crayons and creams can be used to decorate almost any surface, except fabrics that require frequent washing. If the surface has a slight sheen or gloss, apply a spray sealer after you've finished stenciling. This forces the paint to set or cure.

### FABRIC PAINTS

In contrast to acrylic paints, fabric paints remain soft and flexible after drying. Most require the application of heat—either with an iron or a hair dryer—to set the paint (more or less permanently) so it can endure laundering. There are several brands and types of fabric paint on the market, so check labels to make sure that what you buy will work with your particular fabric.

To ensure a long life for your fabric prints, you must first evaluate the suitability of the fabric itself, as certain textures and fibers are not recommended for stenciling and should be avoided. Also, because all prints gradually fade with repeated washings, the paint must be slowly worked into the fibers; if it is only lightly "dusted" on the surface of the fabric the print will fade much more rapidly. For more information on fabric preparation, paint application, and laundering, see "Fabrics," page 78.

You can also use fabric paints to stencil other types of surfaces, but unless you're stenciling on paper you must protect your completed design with varnish or another transparent finish.

*Stenciling paints are available in several forms (from back row, left to right): spray paints and stenciling crayons, japan paints and fluid acrylics, and solid stenciling creams.*

### CERAMIC PAINTS

There are two types of ceramic paints, which are used to decorate smooth, glossy surfaces. *Ceramic studio paints* are formulated for glazed or unglazed ceramic tiles. After firing, these paints become permanent and can withstand day-to-day use and regular cleaning when tiles are installed on floors, countertops, or in showers. *Acrylic enamel paints* are intended for already installed glazed ceramic tiles and glass or ceramic vases or lamps. Once dry, these paints can be wiped with a damp cloth but can't endure vigorous scrubbing. When working with acrylic enamels, you must clean your brushes and stencils immediately or these quick-drying paints will ruin your tools.

### SPRAY PAINTS AND AIRBRUSH

Although their effects are somewhat different, spray paints and airbrush use the same method of application and require the same precautions. While a spray-painted stencil print is delicately dappled and an airbrushed one is softly blended, both methods build color slowly by means of a fine spray. Stenciled spray paint and airbrush prints are quite beautiful, and with some experience and painstaking preparation can be achieved very quickly and easily, but involve significant investments of time and—particularly for airbrush—money.

First and foremost, the fine mists and toxic fumes they produce require that goggles and a respirator or safety mask be worn at all times. Also, all surrounding surfaces must be carefully masked to prevent overspray. Finally, in addition to the airbrush itself, you must also purchase a compressor and special airbrush-compatible inks or paints. Because these considerations can overwhelm even the most intrepid beginner, spray paint and airbrush should be regarded as alternatives for the seasoned stenciler.

Spray paints and airbrush can be used on walls, floors, metals, plastics and fabrics. For more information, see "Stenciling with Airbrush," page 106.

### BLOCKING GLAZES

These translucent glazes are formulated specifically for use with block-printing techniques (see page 39). Their gel-like consistency and reflective properties dramatically illustrate the differences between a paint and a glaze. When executed with opaque paints, block prints look flat and unappealing, but glazes permit the color of the background to show through, giving them depth and dimension. Blocking glazes can also be applied with a pouncing motion on a traditional stencil, and used for faux finishes such as rag-rolling and sponging.

## BRUSHES AND APPLICATORS

Historically, stencilers have used whatever materials are available to apply paint, including sea sponges, wool, even cut and carved potatoes (for block printing). Today, several types of brushes and applicators are made specifically for stenciling. Depending on how they are used, each produces a different kind of print, from vibrant and opaque to dappled and transparent.

### STENCIL BRUSHES

Many stencilers favor traditional stencil brushes, whose short, dense bristles are designed to distribute paint evenly and prevent it from oozing beneath the stencil. This type of brush produces two classic stencil effects: a circular motion produces an even shading, and a pouncing motion yields a light stippling.

Though they vary in size as well as in bristle length, density, and degree of softness, most stenciling brushes are made of hog's hair or boar's hair bristles at least 1 inch long. Their handles are round or tube-shaped, and the bristles are all the same length. The bristles of high-quality stenciling brushes are flagged or split to provide maximum paint hold and distribution.

If you can't find brushes made specifically for stenciling, it is possible to adapt a variety of other brushes. Paint supply companies offer multi-purpose brushes with stiff bristles that can be trimmed and taped into a circular form. Inexpensive shaving brushes can also be used if you intend to use the pouncing technique.

So that you won't have to stop stenciling to clean a brush and let it dry completely before working with another color, it's a good idea to use a separate brush for each color or color family and to have a selection of sizes available. After completing each project or stenciling session, always clean your brushes following the manufacturer's instructions, making sure that no residual pigment remains on the bristles.

### SPONGES

A wedge of cellulose sponge or a piece of natural sea sponge can serve as an inexpensive and disposable stenciling tool. Lightly dab the sponge into the paint, blot it on a paper towel, then pounce or rub the sponge over the stencil window. While a sponge can be used to quickly daub a shaded print or create a dappled background texture, it is not as manageable as a stencil brush, especially when defining the edges of a motif.

A recent addition to the stenciler's toolbox is the sponge-tipped applicator, which is a soft foam sponge attached to a stick. These applicators are inexpensive, reusable, and offer the stenciler yet another textural option. One of their advantages is that they can be rinsed, towel dried, and then used while still slightly damp. In contrast, stencil brushes must be thoroughly cleaned and allowed to dry completely before they can be used again.

### STENCIL ROLLERS

Stencil rollers, which are made of a dense foam, are valued by experienced stencilers for two reasons: They create prints of unusually delicate shading that cannot be achieved with a brush, and they cover large areas quickly. Rollers can also be used to apply the larger primary elements of a stencil, with subsequent overlays applied with brushes. Keep in mind that you'll tend to use more paint because these rollers are so absorbent. Since you'll be applying more paint than you would with a brush or a sponge, you might want to consider using a spray adhesive on back of the stencil. This product holds the stencil more firmly against the surface, giving the edges of the motifs more definition.

### Wool
Wool was one of the first stenciling applicators, and many stencilers today use wool to produce soft, subtle prints. Wrap a strip of 100-percent untreated wool around your index and middle fingers, lightly dab it into paint, blot it on a cloth, then gently rub and pounce it into the stencil window. (If you're working with oil paints, wear tight-fitting disposable surgical gloves to avoid having to clean your hands with turpentine later.)

The type of wool appropriate for stenciling is not easy to find, even in fabric stores. Garage and tag sales are good sources for wool blankets, whose availability today is limited.

### Die-cut Blocks
Block printing (also known as *reverse stenciling*) uses the positive form of a motif—the part that is cut away from a traditional stencil to make a window—to create a loose, freeform design with subtle dimensional shading. Printing blocks can be cut from a variety of materials, including sponges, potatoes, and other vegetables and fruits, by either carving them into simple geometric shapes or using their natural contours. Recently, several companies have introduced die-cut reverse stencil blocks made from a neoprene-type rubber, a flexible, durable material.

## Miscellaneous Equipment
There are several other items that a stenciler should have on hand. These reflect the entire stenciling process, from conception through application.

- *When designing your own stencils* (see page 20), you'll want to work out your ideas on sketch paper. Use a pencil so you can quickly make revisions as your image takes shape.
- *When tracing or adapting a design* from another source, you'll need tracing paper. Use masking tape to firmly attach the original and the tracing paper to your work surface.
- *When positioning a stencil,* use a light-colored chalk pencil for marking the position of repeat lines, a ruler or straightedge to align the pattern repeats, and masking tape or repositionable spray adhesive to fasten the stencil in place.
- *When painting a stencil,* make sure you have the appropriate solvent to maintain the consistency of your paint, correct mistakes, and clean brushes and stencils. Keep plenty of paper towels handy.

*In addition to stenciling brushes, sea sponges, sponge applicators, and stencil rollers can be used to apply paint.*

# DESIGNING AND CUTTING YOUR OWN STENCILS

The materials used to make stencils are as varied as the era and culture in which stenciling is used. Virtually any material can be used to create a stencil if it will effectively mask a precise area of background. A stencil can be created with masking tape, paper doilies, fabric or paper lace, or even natural objects such as leaves or petals.

As your stenciling skills develop and you become accustomed to manipulating color and design within a precut stencil, you will probably want to cut your own. If you don't feel comfortable creating a stencil from scratch, you can consult the many publications that contain copyright-free designs and either trace or adapt one of those patterns. A few words of caution: It is an infringement of copyright to trace a precut stencil pattern, or to copy or adapt the design of a fabric or wallpaper for use other than in your own home.

The most common materials used to make original stencils are acetate, Mylar, and stencil board, all of which are thick enough to be cut and still support an accurate shape. Adele Bishop was the first stenciler to use Mylar (generically referred to as polyester film), which is compatible with both oil- and water-based paints and whose transparency makes it easier to align overlays and repeats.

## SUPPLIES

- *For measuring repeats:* A ruler
- *For the stencil:* Mylar (4 or 5 mil, single matte) *or* E-Z Cut Plastic from P. J. Tetreault *or* stencil board
- *For tracing the design:* A fine-tip permanent marking pen (for transparent stencils) *or* carbon paper and a pencil (for opaque stencils)
- *A cutting surface:* A piece of glass (12 × 14 × ¼ inch, with sanded or covered edges) *or* a "self-healing" PVC cutting mat
- *For cutting the stencil:* A craft or utility knife with replacement blades *or* an electric stencil cutter with a curved tip
- *For repairing the stencil:* Masking tape for stencil board *or* Scotch Invisible tape for acetate or Mylar

## TRACING THE DESIGN

1. Measure the length of the *repeat* (a single set of motifs that, when aligned side by side, will create a continuous, orderly sequence) and the number of overlays that it requires. Dividing a stencil design among several overlays is recommended if more than one color will be used, if the stencil has many small or delicately cut windows, or if a theorem or bridgeless stencil is desired.
2. Position your transparent stencil material over the stencil pattern and tape them both securely in place, making sure to leave at least a 1-inch border of stencil material on all sides of the design.

    If you're working with opaque stencil board, you must either transfer the design to the board by tracing the motifs over a piece of carbon paper, or you can simply affix the design for a single overlay to the board, cut windows through both, and remove the design once you're done.

3. Using a marking pen, trace the design or motif on the transparent stencil material. If the design requires overlays, trace the motifs that will be cut from that particular overlay in solid lines, and use dotted lines for the motifs that will appear on the others. These lines are used during stenciling to accurately align the various motifs as each is painted. The use of a light table is recommended for multiple overlays to ensure the accuracy of the tracings.

    For stencil board, trace the motifs for each overlay with solid lines and a small portion of an adjacent motif from the preceding overlay with dotted lines. While applying paint, you will use this window to align motifs.

4. Continue to trace until all the elements in the design are accounted for. Number and mark the top edge of each sheet with a registration guideline so that sequence, placement, and position will be accurate.

## CUTTING THE STENCIL

Assemble your supplies and *relax*. Don't try to cut your first stencil when you're pressed for time or expect to be interrupted. If you feel nervous about cutting, practice first on a copy of the pattern or on the pattern itself after you've finished tracing so you can make your mistakes there. Your cutting skills will quickly improve with practice.

Before purchasing an electric stencil cutter, most stencilers learn to cut stencils with a utility knife. Note that an electric cutter works best with E-Z Cut Plastic, leaving very few ridges behind, but won't cut through stencil board's waxy coating.

Remember, cut only on the solid black lines, trying to divide them directly in half. Do *not* cut the dotted lines; these will serve as your guides to registration and alignment.

### CUTTING WITH A UTILITY KNIFE

You will find that the cutting technique described below is probably the exact opposite of what you *want* to do, which is to trace the motifs with the utility knife as if you were holding a pencil. You must resist your instinct to do this. It will take some practice to get both hands working together, but this method ensures the highest degree of success.

1. Sit in a chair whose height is comfortable for you at your work surface, and make sure you have adequate lighting. Position your cutting surface directly in front of you.
2. Hold your utility or art knife as you would a pencil and rest the heel of your hand on the cutting surface. Start by cutting a simple shape, applying enough pressure so that the tip of the blade cuts through the stencil and makes contact with the cutting surface.

3. Working very slowly, inch the blade *toward* you. To prevent your cutting hand from wavering or floating above the stencil window, keep the heel of your hand on the cutting surface. You should only use your fingers to move the knife. At the same time, use your other hand to slowly move the stencil so that you are *always* cutting toward yourself.

4. Do not lift the tip of the knife blade until an entire shape has been cut. When you come to a point or a curve, lift the heel of the hand so you can turn the stencil material.

5. When you reach the point where you started cutting, turn the stencil so that your blade is in its original position. This eliminates any little snags that might be present, and the shape should pop out.

### Cutting with an Electric Stencil Cutter

An electric cutter perforates a stencil by means of a heated cutting tip. The efficiency and ease of handling of electric stencil cutters have improved considerably in recent years.

Many models now feature comfortable grips, thermostat controls, and curved copper cutting tips. Note, however, that not all stencil materials can be cut smoothly with an electric cutter. If you find that it leaves ridges within the windows of your acetate or Mylar, try cutting on the gloss side of the sheet.

As with a utility knife, you should practice using the electric cutter on scraps before applying it to your stencil. Its cutting tip can be moved in any direction, making it possible to cut the design with a tracing motion, but it is more difficult to control when moved in a straight horizontal or vertical path.

1. Place the traced stencil on your cutting surface.

2. Apply a uniform pressure to the tip of the cutter. (Too much pressure will bend the tip and too little will prevent it from cutting through the stencil material.)

3. As if you were holding a pencil, trace the motif by moving around the shape. When you come to a point or a juncture in the motif, lift the cutter's tip from the stencil. Do *not* hold the tip in place when rotating on a corner.

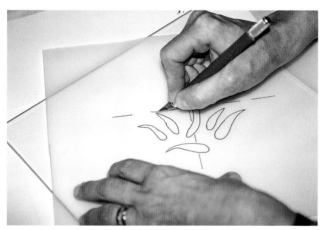

*Resting the heel of your hand on your work surface, hold your utility knife as you would a pencil and begin to cut the stencil by inching the blade toward you. With the other hand, turn the stencil as you cut so that the blade of the knife is always facing you.*

*When you come to a point or curve, lift the heel of your hand so you can turn the stencil.*

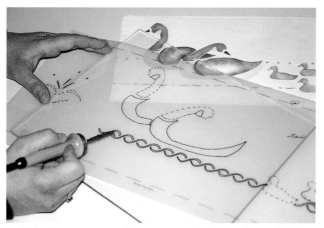

*Hold the electric cutter as if it were a pencil and trace the motif by moving it over its outline.*

## CORRECTING MISTAKES

After you've made all your cuts and evaluated your work, you may find that you've made a few errors. For example, the edges of some of the windows may be uneven, you may not have followed some of the cutting lines exactly, or you may have cut through a bridge or two. You can make adjustments and corrections by doing the following:

- If your windows are incorrectly shaped, you can trim the stencil with a utility knife. If you're right handed, place the area to be trimmed to the *left* of the cutting blade. (If you're left handed, just reverse the stencil-to-blade position.) Moving the knife toward you, trim the stencil window, removing a tiny sliver at a time.

- If you've veered only slightly inside or outside a cutting line, it doesn't necessarily mean that you should reshape the window. You can easily distort a shape even more by trimming and retrimming. Besides, such an "imperfection" is part of the personal touch that goes into cutting a stencil by hand. Before you discard the stencil, you might want to apply paint through the window in question to determine just how problematic it is.

- If you're creating a bridgeless or theorem stencil, you must make sure that the shapes in each overlay fit precisely against each other. Again, some experimentation is needed before you begin stenciling: If a line or bridge is visible in your sample print, go back and trim the stencils on the appropriate overlay(s) to remove it.

- If in the process of cutting or handling a stencil you tear a bridge, simply affix Scotch Invisible tape to both sides of the bridge and recut the window to remove any excess.

## PRACTICE DESIGN

Practice makes perfect! See page 129 for a simple, three-color stencil pattern that even a novice can cut successfully while working to improve his or her technique.

1. On the first overlay, trace the stems and leaves of the flower, as well as the vertical and horizontal registration marks.
2. On the second overlay, mark the motifs from Stencil #1 with dotted lines and trace the petals of the tulip with a solid line.
3. On the third overlay, mark the motif from Stencil #2 with dotted lines and trace the berries with a solid line.
4. As you remove the overlays from the tracing, identify them as Stencil #3, #2, and #1. This step ensures that the overlays are stenciled in the proper sequence.
5. Cut each overlay on the solid lines only.
6. Print the stencil on practice paper to evaluate the quality of your work. Make corrections or adjustments as needed.

*Practice design: Begin by tracing the motifs of the first overlay in solid lines, then add registration marks.*

*On the second overlay, trace the motifs from Stencil #1 and the registration lines with dotted lines and trace the petals of the tulip with solid lines. Complete the third overlay, identify each one for proper sequence, then carefully cut the stencils.*

# ADAPTING A STENCIL FROM AN EXISTING DESIGN

Not surprisingly, you'll discover that inspiration for your original stencil designs can spring from many sources. In most instances, your stenciling decisions will depend on the decor of the room you'd like to stencil. If the room is just beginning to take shape and contains little in the way of draperies, furniture, and other restrictive details, you're pretty much free to develop the decor—and your stencil design—in practically any direction. On the other hand, if the decor of a room is well established, or if you plan to design an environment in which all the elements share the same or comparable motifs or colors, you may want to adapt the design of a wallpaper, fabric, or even an object, such as a vintage print or a piece of antique china.

Because stenciled images are composed of a system of windows and bridges, adapting a stencil from a secondary source usually involves a process of simplification (the reduction of an image into segments) and isolation (choosing one or a few motifs from among many). In the example shown below, Jan Demerath adapted a fabric design ("Rhapsody" by Croscill) through such a process.

The width of the wallpaper border that she had ordered to match her comforter and draperies seemed to overpower the room. Jan dissected the border by cutting out the main floral forms, then distributed them more loosely to give the design an open, airy look. Jan eventually reduced the various colors in each flower and leaf to two. Overall the stenciled border is less elaborate than the original, yet still complements the decor beautifully.

The dull, flat finish of the textured walls provided an excellent surface for stenciling. Jan cut this stencil with a pair of manicure scissors, whose curved contours were just right for the arched motifs. She applied acrylic paints with stencil brushes, finishing selected elements with highlights designed to visually diminish the texture of the wall. Immediately after stenciling a repeat, Jan loaded a brush with white paint and highlighted the centers of larger cutout areas. This can be done easily after the stencil has been removed. Jan also recommends using disposable baby wipes for removing water-based paint from walls. (For more information on avoiding and correcting mistakes, see page 35.)

*Jan began by cutting the wallpaper border apart to select a few design elements, then rearranged them until she had a pleasing layout.*

*The completed stencil border coordinates with the lively floral pattern of the draperies without detracting from them. Designed, adapted, and stenciled by Jan Demerath.*

*The loose, free-flowing style of block printing, a type of stenciling that uses positive forms to create images (see page 39), has contributed to its recent surge in popularity. Designed and block-printed by Jane Gauss and Liza Glenn for Plaid Enterprises. Courtesy of Plaid Enterprises, Inc.*

# BASIC TECHNIQUES

Before you can tackle your first stenciling project, you must have an understanding of basic application techniques. Armed with this information, you can then consider the variables specific to your project. The step-by-step photographs in this chapter are designed to help the first-time stenciler get started, and to ensure success even on the first attempt. If you have some stenciling experience, you may find some suggestions that can improve your style or technique.

After you've read through the instructions for applying each type of paint, begin by experimenting with different paints and techniques. Regardless of your level of experience, experimentation will enable you to develop your own style, so that all of your stencil designs and prints bear the mark of your unique brand of creativity. It's encouraging to remember that the stencilers whose work is featured in this book were all beginners at one time, and that some day your work will motivate and instruct others.

# STENCILING WITH LIQUID PAINTS

When working with liquid paints, maintaining their consistency is the most important part of the stenciling procedure. Although the recommended paint consistency is that of heavy cream, there is no "ideal" that you must work to achieve. Instead, you must determine what is appropriate for a particular project, as long as paint buildup on stencils and applicators is minimal.

Regardless of the type of paint used for stenciling, the techniques and tools for application remain the same. It is important to remember, however, that if you use a paint that is not formulated specifically for stenciling, such as an interior house paint with a high degree of coverage, it can be difficult to achieve delicately shaded prints or to clean your stenciling tools adequately.

## SUPPLIES
- *For stirring paint:* craft sticks *or* palette knives
- *For maintaining paint consistency and rejuvenating applicators:* extender or isopropyl rubbing alcohol for acrylic paints *or* turpentine or mineral spirits for japan paints
- *For loading the applicator:* a flat plastic plate
- *An applicator:* brush *or* sponge applicator
- *For blotting the applicator:* paper towels (use an absorbent brand)
- *For affixing the stencil:* low-tack masking tape *or* repositionable adhesive

## MAINTAINING PAINT CONSISTENCY
In general, paint is at the proper consistency for stenciling when it is first taken from a newly opened container. It requires thinning only when it is exposed to the air, either after it has been poured onto the palette or applicator-loading surface or if the container is left open. (Note that certain conditions, such as extreme heat or the draft from an open window, can cause paint to cure more rapidly.) Use isopropyl rubbing alcohol or extender to thin acrylics, and turpentine or mineral spirits to thin japan paints. The following are some general guidelines for maintaining a workable paint consistency.

- Stir the paints thoroughly in their containers, making sure to incorporate any pigments that have settled to the bottom. Shaking the container will not mix the paint completely, especially if it has already been opened and sitting on the shelf for some time.
- Place approximately 1 teaspoon of paint on the plate at a time. The paint should be the consistency of heavy cream. As it thickens, it will become gummy and quickly build up on the applicator and stencil. Mist the paint lightly or add thinner *one drop at a time,* then stir the paint thoroughly.
- Do *not* thin paints to a runny consistency. This will make it difficult to sufficiently blot the paint from your applicator, resulting in a wet, smudged print.

## LOADING THE APPLICATOR
Even when stenciled prints are bold and opaque, stenciling is always done with a *drybrush technique.* This means that very little paint is used and that color and shading are built up gradually, resulting in a very smooth, defined edge.

1. When the paint is mixed to a workable consistency, hold the applicator perpendicular to the plate, then place it into the paint and twist it as if you were driving in a screw. This loads the paint into the center of the applicator without smearing it on its outer bristles or surface. Remove the applicator from the paint.
2. At this point, the applicator is loaded with far too much paint to begin stenciling. Try to remove all of the paint from the applicator by rubbing it into or blotting it on a paper towel. Hold or tape the paper towel securely to your work surface, then make several circular strokes with the applicator. Finally, make an X stroke on the towel to remove any paint that remains on the applicator's outer bristles or surface.
3. Using masking tape or repositionable adhesive, attach the stencil to the surface, glossy side up.
4. Hold the applicator in your hand as you would a pencil, tilting it so that its tip is perpendicular to the surface. Although it may seem that you've already removed all of the paint from the applicator, you must always test the consistency of the remaining paint *before* stenciling. Daub your applicator on an uncut margin of the stencil. If a wet smudge is left behind, there is still too much paint on the applicator. Wipe the applicator on a paper towel, then test it again on the uncut part of the stencil. When the stroke no longer appears wet, you can begin stenciling.

## APPLYING THE PAINT
As you apply paint within a stencil window, you must concentrate your vision on the uncut surface surrounding it rather than on filling in the shape. The technical term for this visualization technique is called *focus of vision,* and it applies to all types of paint and stenciling techniques. By concentrating on the area around the windows, the edges of the shapes are defined more effectively, and the paint is distributed more evenly within each motif and accumulates less quickly on the stencil.

1. Using either a pouncing motion or a circular stroke, apply the paint within the stencil window. Keep the applicator perpendicular to the surface at all times by locking your wrist and moving your entire arm. Do *not* use a sweeping stroke. Start with a light stroke, and as the paint is released from the applicator, slowly increase the pressure. As you work the applicator in first a clockwise, then a counterclockwise motion, hold the stencil in place with your other hand to keep the paint from seeping beneath it.
2. Lift the corner of the stencil from time to time to evaluate the depth of color and to check for sharp, crisp edges on each motif. It's much easier to darken a print than to lighten it, so it's best to work slowly. To darken a

motif, do not immediately reload the applicator; simply increase pressure in order to continue to release paint from its center. Only reload the applicator when you can no longer discharge color from it.

## REJUVENATING THE APPLICATOR

Before reloading, you must first *rejuvenate the applicator.* This procedure maintains the applicator's flexibility (especially the dense bristles of a stencil brush) and reduces paint buildup on the stencil. This "clean-as-you-go" approach makes the stenciling process much faster and easier, since you'll have to stop to clean your tools much less often. Clean a transparent stencil when you can no longer see through it, or when paint that's built up around the windows makes the edges of the print look messy and ill-defined.

1. Dampen the center of a piece of paper towel folded into quarters with approximately 1 teaspoon of solvent (isopropyl rubbing alcohol for acrylics, *or* mineral spirits or turpentine for japan paints), then pull the applicator

through the solvent. *Never* immerse an applicator in solvent, and do *not* use water, even if you're working with water-based paints. The solvent evaporates quickly enough to keep the applicator from becoming soggy.

2. Return to the stencil. Using a circular motion, work the applicator on the area *surrounding* the window. (Do *not* insert the applicator inside the window, as this will cause the stenciled motif to streak.) The solvent in the applicator will pick up the paint that was left on the stencil during the first application.

## RELOADING THE APPLICATOR

Before reloading, test the consistency of the paint on the plate. Chances are that it has thickened slightly, even if you're working quickly. If necessary, review the guidelines above for maintaining paint consistency. Add a drop of solvent to the paint or mist it with a pump sprayer. Make sure that the paint is the consistency of heavy cream—or the same consistency it was for the initial loading—before reloading.

1

2

3

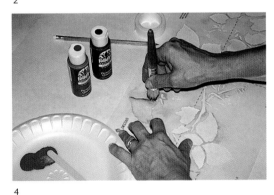

4

5

6

1. Hold the applicator perpendicular to the plate, dip it into the paint, and twist it with a screwing motion.
2. Stroke the freshly loaded applicator on a clean paper towel to remove excess paint.
3. Before stenciling, test the consistency of the paint on the applicator by daubing it on an uncut portion of the stencil.
4. While applying the paint, focus your vision on the surface of the stencil immediately surrounding the window.
5. Lift the stencil to evaluate the print's depth of color and the definition of its edges.
6. To rejuvenate your applicator, draw it through a paper towel dampened with the appropriate solvent.

# APPLYING LIQUID PAINT WITH A STENCIL ROLLER

As demonstrated by Sandra and Linda Buckingham at a recent Stencil Artisans League convention, stencil rollers apply paint remarkably quickly and produce shaded prints of exceptional subtlety.

For their presentation, Sandra and Linda used a dense foam roller, interior wall paint, and a stencil cut from 5-mil polyester film. You can stencil with a foam roller using any type of liquid paint, but keep in mind that a roller absorbs more paint than a brush or a sponge. A dense foam roller is more suitable for stenciling than a standard paint roller, which is designed to soak up as much paint as possible.

When used with interior wall paint, a roller can become particularly gummy if exposed to air too long. To "rejuvenate" your roller, roll it over a moist paper towel dampened with water, and wrap it in plastic wrap or aluminum foil if you plan to take a break for more than a few minutes. When you've finished stenciling for the day, clean your roller with soap and water.

Before you begin, review the instructions on page 26 for maintaining paint consistency.

1. Work the roller into the paint. Blot the roller twice—first on brown paper, then on paper toweling—until most of the paint is removed. (You need to roll off excess paint just as you would with a brush—it's still basically a "drybrush" technique.) This allows you to work quickly and get an even coat.
2. Pressing lightly, apply the roller to the entire stencil first in one direction, then another. Increase the pressure as the paint begins to adhere to the surface. The stencil is complete in just a fraction of the time it takes to apply paint with a brush or sponge.
3. If desired, shade the motifs with a brush or sponge.

1. Load the roller with paint, then blot it on brown paper.

2. Blot the roller again on paper toweling.

3. Roll the entire stencil first in one direction, then another.

4. Check the print for color and definition. A stencil roller produces a sharp print much more rapidly than other applicators.

5. Shade the motifs with a brush or sponge if desired.

6. The completed stencil-roller print. Designed and stenciled by Sandra and Linda Buckingham.

# STENCILING WITH SOLID PAINTS

As is the case with many of the paints now used with stenciling, solid paints were originally developed for use by fine artists or for other crafts. Many of the new generation of solid paint crayons and creams designed specifically for stenciling offer blendability and permanence (even on fabrics) without the bother of dirty stencils or run-under prints.

   Because paint consistency among brands is so similar, you can mix and match paints from several manufacturers, making a large and varied palette easily obtainable. Just make sure that the base of the paints is the same, either water *or* oil, *never* both. Follow the manufacturer's instructions for cleanup.

## WORKING WITH STICK PAINTS OR STENCIL CRAYONS

The word "crayon" can easily mislead stencilers into thinking that they can use a stick of solid paint to color in a window directly, something you should never do. Instead, think of a stencil stick or crayon as a container of paint, which is essentially what it is. This means that, as with liquid paints, you need a palette or loading surface on which to deposit the paint, and an area to work the paint into the applicator. The circular stroke used to load the paint onto the applicator is the means by which the solid paint is converted into a liquid. Once these steps have been taken, stencil crayons can be used to produce both opaque and shaded prints.

1. A new solid paint crayon or stick is sealed with a wax coating that must be removed before it can be used. Gently peel away the coating or make several X strokes with the crayon on a paper towel. Discard the wax seal.
2. Using either an uncut part of the stencil or a nonabsorbent surface such as a piece of aluminum foil or waxed freezer paper as a palette, stroke the stencil crayon directly on its surface.
3. Work the applicator into the paint with a circular stroke, then stroke it on another surface to disperse the paint into it.
4. Hold the applicator perpendicular to the stencil, then apply the paint into the window with a circular or pouncing motion.

*Remove the wax seal from the stick or crayon with a paper towel.*

*Apply some paint to the uncut part of the stencil or onto a separate loading surf then load it onto the applicator.*

*Work the paint into the bristles or the surface of the applicator.*

## WORKING WITH STENCIL CREAMS

The consistency of stencil cream paints is similar to that of cream blush or lipstick. Stencil cream prints look very similar to those made with stencil crayons or stick paints.

1. Remove the skim coat from the paint by wiping it with a paper towel. As these paints are "self-sealing," this coating will form after any period of disuse, so you'll need to remove it every time you reopen the container.

2. Load an applicator by wiping it directly into the paint. Disperse the paint into the applicator by rubbing it on the border of the stencil or another paint-loading surface. Blot the applicator only to remove any globs of paint, which usually means that the paint hasn't been manipulated properly with the applicator or that there was too much paint on the applicator to begin with.

3. Hold the brush perpendicular to the stencil, then apply the paint into the window with a circular or pouncing motion.

*Remove the skim coat from the surface of the paint with a paper towel.*

*Load the brush by stroking it directly into the paint.*

*A completed solid stencil paint print. Stencil crayons and creams both yield prints of soft, subtle shading with sharp, crisp edges.*

# STENCIL PRINT SAMPLER

The stencil prints below and on the opposite page illustrate
the range of values and textures that can be achieved
simply by varying or combining the tools and methods of
paint application.

*A traditional drybrush print in acrylic paints
applied with a stencil brush in a circular
stroke, showing very smooth, controlled edges.
Blue Laser stencil by American Traditional.*

*Acrylic paint applied with a brush using a
combination of circular and pouncing
techniques.*

*Acrylic paint pounced on with a sponge
wedge.*

*Acrylic paint swirled, pounced, and dabbed
on with a sponge applicator on a stick.*

*Liquid paint lightly loaded on a sponge applicator and applied in a wiping motion. Stencil by American Home.*

*An opaque print stenciled with stencil crayons applied with a brush. Each set of motifs was shaded with a second color. Stencil designed by Deb Mores.*

*Stencil creams applied with a brush to produce dark-to-light shading, from the edges to each motif to its center. Stencil designed by Melanie Royals.*

# AVOIDING AND CORRECTING MISTAKES

The key to a successful stencil project is planning, and a little preparation goes a long way in preventing major problems. With that said, it should be noted that very few errors can't be corrected, and that what you know is a "mistake" might very well be perceived as an integral part of the design or go unnoticed by virtually everyone else.

## BRUSH-UNDERS AND RUN-UNDERS

*Brush-unders* (also called *run-unders*) are smudges of paint that extend beneath the window of an individual motif. Brush-unders occur when the bristles of a brush slip beneath the surface of the stencil during application, or when the stencil is not secured tightly enough to the stenciling surface. Run-unders are caused by paint seeping under a stencil, either because the paint is too runny or the stencil is not flush against the stenciling surface. Always tape the stencil in place and press it tightly to the surface while applying paint. Repositionable spray adhesive is more reliable than tape for ensuring that your stencils stay in place.

The following are a few suggestions for correcting brush-unders and run-unders when stenciling walls, ceilings, and other flat, repaintable surfaces:

- If the smudge is very slight, use a kneaded artist's eraser to remove it. It's generally not necessary to wait until a print has dried completely to make corrections, but you should at least let the paint set up first. If necessary, blot minor smudges with a paper towel or cotton swab moistened with the appropriate solvent.
- If the smudge is more conspicuous or can't be removed with a kneaded eraser, shift the stencil so that the window overlaps the smudged area and paint over it, or use another part of the stencil to cover it with another motif.
- For really big smudges, repaint the surface, let dry, and restencil.

If you're working on fabric, wood, or other surfaces with special considerations, refer to "Other Stenciling Projects," pages 70–103, for specific instructions.

## PAPER PROOFS

A *paper proof* is sample print made on a sheet of paper prior to stenciling. It is an invaluable tool that can save you hours of frustration. Use a paper proof to check the following:

- *The accuracy of overlays and alignment of repeats.* A paper proof is particularly effective for evaluating stencils of your own design. You will see whether you cut the windows precisely, or if any of your cutting errors are discernible in the print. A paper proof also serves as a tool for measuring repeats, particularly when stenciling a wall border into corners, and for understanding the flow of a design. (See "Measuring and Laying Out Borders," page 49.)
- *Paint color, value, and intensity.* You should make more than one proof—three or four are suggested—to evaluate these variables, as well as variations in paint, tools, and application. To assess color intensity accurately, paint the paper with the background color of the wall or object before proofing a stencil. The background color will have a significant impact on the overall effect of the design, so don't leave out this important first step.

Before you commit to any treatment, wait at least a day or two and live with your proofs. For instance, if you're proofing a wall border, tape the proofs to the wall of the actual room at the border's approximate height. Appraise them in the context of the existing decor and furnishings, both in daylight and artificial light. Use one of the prints—or, if necessary, specific areas from each print—as the model for your project, and refer to it throughout the stenciling process.

For borders and large designs, the backs of computer spreadsheets work quite well for proofing. You can use leftover wallpaper by painting it with the background color of your project (or just plain white) to cover the pattern. The unwaxed side of 24-inch-wide freezer paper is another option. Blank newsprint's poor absorbency and dull color make it an unwise choice.

*The green motifs in this print show an uneven application of paint and poor focus of vision. Continue proofing your stencil on paper until you're pleased with the results, then use the proof as a guide for color, value, and intensity.*

# CREATING DIMENSION WITH COLOR AND VALUE

As you can see from the stencil print sampler on pages 32–33, you can suggest depth and dimension within a print simply by varying a single color's value. *Value* is the relative lightness or darkness of a color, as it relates to white (the highest value), black (the lowest value), and the range of grays in between. Pink, for example, is a high-value red, while maroon is a low-value red.

The ways in which color and value are used in a stencil design are primarily based on personal preference. There are several approaches to consider. You can:

- Paint each motif with one flat, opaque color. This is often done in so-called "primitive-style" prints based on 18th-century and early 19th-century designs, and in simple modern designs.

- Shade each motif from dark (around the edges) to light (near the centers) with one color, or place a mask over a uniform application of color to darken specific areas.
- Moderate the values of similarly colored motifs to suggest depth by varying pressure during application. With this technique, darker petals within a flower will appear closer, while lighter ones will appear further away.
- Shade selected motifs with one or more other colors. This is called *overprinting*.

Experiment with all these effects, then try combining them in a single print. You'll find that the character and the content of the stencil itself, as well as the decor of your room, will influence your decisions about color, highlighting, and shading.

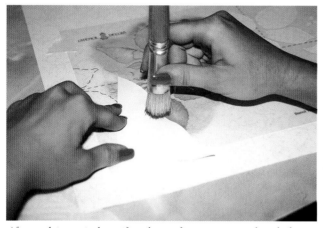

After applying a single, uniform layer of paint, use a mask to darken specific areas of the leaves.

The shaded print. The position of the mask can be easily adjusted so that the contours of the shading are soft and natural-looking.

This lovely wisteria print was stenciled in two colors of paint, and with overlays a multi-shaded print was produced. Stencil designed by Decorative Arts Studio.

This ivy design shows another type of shading. By moving the flower cluster stencil slightly and stenciling with a very light touch, the flower cluster looks much larger and depth is added to the print. Stencil designed by Deb Mores.

This lamb was stenciled in gray acrylic, then shaded with black. This type of blending, which is called overprinting, suggests a handpainted look. Stencil designed by Deb Mores.

# STACKING

In addition to the shading effects shown on page 35, the technique known as *stacking* is used to create dimension and depth by overlapping prints. In a stacked stencil print, the first print (which will appear closest to the viewer) is masked with the cutout portion of its stencil, then the second stencil is positioned to overlap it. The cutout portion of the first print is removed, and if the object represented is transparent, the stencil for the second print is replaced and the outline of its "concealed" area is gently painted in.

Although stacking is usually considered an intermediate technique because it is used to create murals and other complex images, Nancy Tribolet demonstrated at a recent Stencil Artisans League workshop that even a beginner can achieve this dimensional style of stenciling. Nancy used solid stencil creams and a soft stencil brush for her presentation.

1. Stencil the item that will appear closest to the viewer first.

2. Cover the first print with the cutout portion of its stencil, then stencil the second print so that its window overlaps the covered first print.

3. Remove the second stencil. The second print will appear to be behind the first.

4. The completed stacked print. Designed and stenciled by Nancy Tribolet.

# FREEFORM AND FREEHAND STENCILING

The designs and repeat patterns of many stencils, particularly borders, are unvarying and fairly rigid. Motifs usually occur at regular intervals and are identically or very similarly positioned. In contrast, *freeform stenciling* uses individual motifs as the building blocks of a design, randomly varying their position, sequence, and orientation according to the stenciler's personal taste and the needs of the room or project. Because of its flexibility, freeform stenciling is often used to highlight or enhance a particular area or feature of a room. This stenciling style is most compatible with design motifs that are innately free-flowing, such as leaves, vines, or flowers, but it can be used with a wide range of others.

*Freehand stenciling* (also called *overpainting*) is the addition of handpainted details to a previously stenciled motif. For example, you might want to add veins to some or all of your leaves, or add pupils or highlights to a teddy bear's eyes. For best results, do your freehand work in a color that contrasts significantly with that of the stenciled motif. Test your color choices on a paper proof to ensure that they make sense visually.

Shown below and on the following page are some examples of freehand stenciling, some of which also include freehand painting. Using eggshell finish latex housepaint on a semi-gloss surface, Sandra Buckingham adapted individual leaf and vine patterns to produce two completely different looks. One is delicately shaded in a lighter green over a darker green background, while the other uses different values and freehand veining in the leaves to suggest depth and dimension.

Sandra also created an elegant cave art bedroom motif with a combination of precut stencils and torn freezer paper masks. First, she loosely applied a rich terra cotta color wash of diluted latex housepaint in all directions so that the intensity of color varied randomly. Next, she measured and taped off the background of the border area with low-tack Kleen Edge tape. She applied the vivid earth colors of the stone's veins and striations with sea sponges and foam rollers, using long, unevenly torn strips of freezer paper to paint the jagged edges between them, occasionally overlapping colors to increase the complexity of the texture. She then stenciled the figures in solid black using stencil brushes and a circular rubbing or swirling technique.

Julia Heirl Burmesch's wreath design makes the most of her sunroom's limited wall space, a result of a high, peaked ceiling and many windows. The rose theme was inspired by the tiny roses in upholstery fabric on wicker furniture, which she also used as a guide to custom-mix acrylic paints. She used smaller brushes (3/8 to 5/8 inch) to maximize speed of application and paint control with the single-piece stencil.

Melanie Royals's freeform stencil sets feature individually cut floral and leaf stencils that can be combined in any number of ways to create one-of-a-kind designs. All of the veins, connecting vines, and tendrils are added freehand with artist's liner brushes and thinned paint, which enhances the handpainted look of the designs.

*These two applications of the same grapevine stencils demonstrate the versatility of using a few individual leaf stencils as the building blocks of a freeform design. They can be combined, overlapped, and shaded to look like meandering vines, clustered branches, or shaped topiary. Stencils from Buckingham Stencils Garden Room Collection; stenciled by Sandra Buckingham.*

This large wreath is composed of a series of single-piece stencils. Designed and stenciled by Julia Hierl Burmesch.

The flowers of these very realistic-looking geraniums are composed of overlapping layers of petal cluster stencils, starting with a dark color and finishing with a lighter color. It always helps to look at a real plant when doing this type of design. Designed and stenciled by Melanie Royals.

Three stencil sets—"Romantic Ribbon Trellis," "Sweetheart Ivy Topiary," and "Sweetheart Rosebud Topiary"—were used to create these stencil prints. Any number of topiary shapes can be created using the topiary stencil sets. The rosebud topiary set comes with a ceramic pot, and the ivy topiary comes with three sizes of clay pots. The ivy and rosebuds can be also be entwined at random through the ribbon trellis. Designed and stenciled by Melanie Royals.

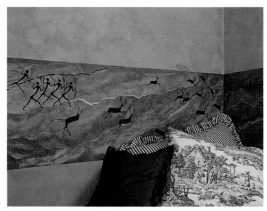

A background created with latex paint, sponges, and freezer paper provides just the right look for these cave painting stencils. Designed and stenciled by Sandra Buckingham.

# BLOCK PRINTING

Dating back to ancient Egypt, block printing (also known as *reverse stenciling*) has been used throughout history for decoration and embellishment. Block printing uses the positive forms of motifs to create an image, whereas traditional stenciling uses their negative, or cutout, shapes.

Even if you're new to stenciling, chances are good that you've made block prints before. (Remember those potato prints you made in elementary school art class?) You can also use sponges and other vegetables and fruits, either by carving them or using their natural cut profiles, to create stunning wall motifs, cascading florals, or twisting vines. Vegetable printing can even be used to make beautiful fabric designs.

Many stencilers block-print with die-cut blocking pads made from a neoprene-type rubber. When used with translucent, gel-like glazes, these pads produce breathtaking prints so easily that even a beginner can achieve professional results.

## Supplies
- *For marking the flow of the design:* ¼-inch quilter's tape *or* a light gray chalk pencil
- Blocking pads
- Blocking glazes
- *For loading the blocks:* a plastic plate *or* a sheet of palette paper
- *Brushes:* flat (for loading the blocks) and round (for finishing the prints)
- *For blotting the loaded blocks:* scrap pieces of brown paper bags
- *For correcting mistakes:* an old terry cloth towel moistened with water

## Notching the Handle (Optional)
Attached to each blocking pad is a short handle that is used to load the block with glaze and to remove it from the printed surface. (Do *not* use this handle to create stems on your leaves.) To prevent glaze from creeping up the handle during loading, you might choose to notch the handle with a sharp craft or utility knife. This step isn't required, but if you skip it you'll have to be extra careful when loading the block so that the handle doesn't get smudged.

1. At the point where the handle meets the block, lightly mark the edge of the natural shape of the blocking pad. On this line, make a cut no deeper than ¹/₁₆ inch.
2. Hold the block face up in your nonwriting hand, then cut a wedge from the handle into the pierced line. It should be a very shallow wedge, just deep enough to define the natural shape of the block.

## Marking the Layout
Using quilter's tape or chalk, mark the flow of the design on the stenciling surface or paper proof. If applicable, follow the natural configuration of the motif you're working with. Keep in mind, for example, that leaves will typically gravitate toward a light source. You can remove the tape or chalk line as your design progresses.

## Loading the Block
1. With the flat brush, evenly apply a moderate amount of glaze to the detailed or cut side of the block.
2. Using the same brush, load the block with several values of color. This produces very natural-looking shading. Note that a moderate load of glaze will produce three to five prints, depending on the porosity of the blocking surface.
3. Before making a print, test the loaded block on a practice sheet of paper. Continue to practice on paper until you feel comfortable with the pressing and lifting procedure described below. If the block slides on the paper, gently blot it on a scrap piece of brown paper bag or a smooth, flat surface. You'll also want to blot your block if you've overloaded it, or if you're block-printing a piece of fabric.

1. Using quilter's tape or light gray chalk, map the general flow of the design.

## MAKING A PRINT

1. Hold the loaded block by the handle with one hand, turn the block over, then lightly press or set it against the surface with the other hand. Release the handle immediately. (Use the handle only to load the block and remove it from the surface.)

2. Press down over the entire surface of the block with your fingertips. To prevent the block from sliding, hold it with the fingers of your left hand while you "walk" the fingers of your right hand around that part of the shape. Repeat with the other hand. This technique prevents the print from looking like it was "rubber-stamped" and allows the glaze to bond to the surface, resulting in a more handpainted look.

3. Remove the block by its handle, then reapply it to the surface to make another print.

4. Position the block for additional prints. With each pressing the color will become progressively lighter, creating natural gradations in color and shading. Because the neoprene is flexible, the block can be rolled so that just a portion of a shape appears "behind" a darker print or shows a motif in profile. Before you overlap prints, make sure the first one has dried.

2. Load each blocking pad with a moderate amount of glaze.

3. If the block is loaded too heavily or if you want a delicate print, blot it on a piece of scrap paper.

4. Set block on the surface to be printed, then release the handle.

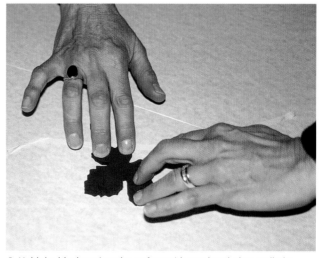

5. Hold the block against the surface with one hand, then walk the fingers of the other around the edge.

## CORRECTING MISTAKES

1. If you make a mistake on a wall or wood surface, remove the glaze with a terry cloth towel slightly moistened with water. If the glaze stains the surface, you can reblock the same area with a lighter load of glaze.

2. Before removing prints that you feel are too dark or are slightly smudged around the edges, stand back and look at your proof to evaluate the overall pattern. Darker prints add depth and dimension to the flow of the design. Before making a correction, consider whether the error is a glaring one, or if it fits into the design as a whole.

## ADDING FINISHING TOUCHES

You don't have to wait for glazes to dry before adding details like vines and tendrils. In fact, it's best to begin working on them immediately after printing a group of motifs.

1. Dip the round brush in neutral glaze, load it with only a hint of the motif color, and moisten it with a drop of water.

2. As you paint the vine or other detail, drag it through the already printed motifs, letting it become fully saturated with glaze.

3. Keeping your wrist loose, use a pulling, twisting motion to lightly connect some of the leaves and flowers.

6. Remove the block by the handle, then print again.

7. You can make three to five prints with each load of glaze. Notice how each successive print is slightly lighter.

8. Using a round brush loaded with neutral glaze and a hint of color, add a hint of connecting vine. Block glazes and blocking pads by Plaid Enterprises.

## VEGETABLE PRINTING

In the step-by-step photographs shown on the opposite page, Carol Lumpkin demonstrates the beauty and simplicity of vegetable printing. You can carve fruits or vegetables into simple shapes like flowers or leaves, or create more sophisticated designs such as vines, berries, fruit garlands, and intricate florals. You can also print with the fruit or vegetable itself, either whole or cut. Vegetable prints are casual, loose, impressionistic, and slightly weathered in appearance.

Some of the best fruits and vegetables to use for printing are also the most common: potatoes, turnips, apples, pears, carrots, cabbage, celery, and artichokes. Acrylic paints work best with fruits and vegetables; most oil-based paints do not mix well with their natural fluids, making printing difficult.

Although the instructions that follow are for a raw cooking potato, you can use any fruit or vegetable you have on hand.

### SUPPLIES

- *For making the print:* a fruit or vegetable of your choice
- *For carving the fruit or vegetable:* a paring knife
- *For loading the carved fruit or vegetable:* an artist's brush and a paper plate *or* palette
- *For proofing the print:* blank newsprint

## CARVING THE POTATO

1. Cut the potato in half, either horizontally or vertically, depending on the amount of printing surface you need. Make a smooth, even cut.
2. On one half of the potato, lightly carve the desired shape into the cut surface.
3. When you are satisfied with your shape, make a deep cut (about 1 inch) straight down into the potato. Continue to cut around the outline of your shape until you've returned to the starting point.
4. From the outside of the potato, cut inward to gently remove sections of potato so that only your shape is left.
5. The printing surface of your potato should project out far enough so that your fingers won't get in the way while you're printing. Make sure that you can hold the potato securely and that it doesn't slip while printing. If necessary, trim the sides of the potato for an easier grip or use a fork for a handle.

### MAKING A PRINT

To print, load the potato with paint by brushing the paint onto the printing surface of the potato or by dipping the potato into the paint. Experiment with both methods. It will take several minutes and several prints before the vegetable will begin to print accurately. Practice on sheets of blank newsprint until you are pleased with the results.

*A "garland of plenty" vegetable print designed and printed by Carol Lumpkin.*

1. Lightly carve the desired shape into the cut surface of the potato.

2. Working from the outside of the potato, cut inward toward the carved outline of the shape, removing sections of the potato as you go.

3. Print your design on the surface to be stenciled.

4. If desired, add small details with an artist's brush.

5. A finished potato print. Designed and printed by Carol Lumpkin.

*The stenciled dado in this dining alcove is based on Slavic embroidery motifs. Its simplified color scheme reduces the complexity of its design so that it complements the decor's other principal element—a Native American throw rug—instead of overpowering it. Designed and stenciled by Adele Bishop.*

# STENCILED INTERIORS

While stenciling is an extremely flexible decorating medium, there are a few basic guidelines to follow when stenciling a room. Perhaps the best advice for first-time stencilers is that they should focus on just one part of a room at a time; for example, a border at the ceiling line. Then, after the furniture and accessories are back in place, you can decide if additional stenciling touches would enhance or detract from the visual balance of the room. You don't need to be a professional decorator to know whether a room's decor feels "comfortable"—when it complements the space perfectly. If each time you walk into a room it seems to shout out, "Look at me—I'm stenciled," it probably means that it wasn't planned carefully. By starting with a little stenciling and then gradually adding more, you can be sure that your room will suit your taste and lifestyle.

# PLANNING A ROOM

Your stenciling should blend with and enhance everything else in a room, from the color of the walls to the fabrics, flooring, and accessories. If a room is completely furnished and accessorized, then select a stencil that will complement rather than conflict with the existing decor. On the other hand, if the room is sparsely furnished and has few or no accessories from which to draw inspiration for color or design, then you can use a more dramatic stencil as the focal point of the room. Evaluate each design within the context of the particular decor or room.

Study the photographs of the stenciled interiors that appear later in this chapter. You'll find a wide range of approaches to color, design, and layout. There are so many decorating and stenciling ideas that you'll learn something new about layout and design each time you look through these pages. Since your first task is to choose a starting point for your stenciling and to consider where and how it can be applied, let these images provide a springboard for your own creativity. So much of stenciling's appeal is derived from the fact that each stenciler can use it to express his or her individuality, creating a completely personal environment.

## DIVIDING A ROOM INTO SECTIONS

Before you begin stenciling a room, you must first consider the stencil design in terms of orientation—horizontal, vertical, and individual or spot motifs. Then divide the room into sections so that the distribution of the stenciling will be balanced. There is a specific sequence of steps to follow when stenciling walls.

### 1. STENCIL ALL HORIZONTALS

A room can have any or all of the following horizontal placements:

- A *frieze* is a border stenciled at the top of a room, positioned approximately 1 inch below the ceiling line or crown molding. If the area above a door or window is not wide enough to utilize the complete border stencil, stencil the portion of the design that will fit, and then continue with the complete design to maintain the flow. Do *not* select a narrow design to accommodate spacing above a door or window. Instead, choose a design that is in proportion with the dimensions of the entire room.
- A *chair rail* or *wainscoting* can be stenciled either 1/2 to 3/4 inch above or below an architectural chair rail, or at the customary height of 32 to 36 inches from the floor.
- A *dado* is stenciled on the lower part of a wall, from below the chair rail to above the base molding.
- A *kickplate* or *mopboard* is stenciled approximately 1/2 to 3/4 inch above the base molding.

### 2. STENCIL ALL VERTICALS

Vertical borders are often used to frame doorways and windows or to divide a wall into stenciled panels. All vertical stencil lines must be stopped by a horizontal line. When stenciling around doors and windows or creating molding panels, first stencil the horizontal, then drop the vertical down to the chair rail or kickplate.

### 3. ADD INDIVIDUAL OR CENTRAL MOTIFS

Central motifs and accessory embellishments are stenciled last. There is no definitive rule as to how these motifs should be placed. Stencil several proofs of the motif and use them to determine the best placement, then maintain the same placement relationships throughout the entire room. For example, an individual motif can be used as a central focal point, or repeated systematically to create a complex wallpaper effect.

*Stencil all horizontal borders first. From Stenciling Your Walls by Jane Gauss, copyright © 1990 by Plaid Enterprises. Courtesy of Plaid Enterprises, Inc.*

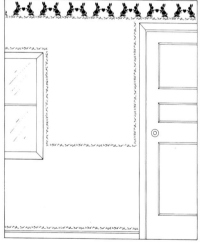

*Stencil all vertical borders second. All verticals must be stopped by a horizontal. From Stenciling Your Walls by Jane Gauss, copyright © 1990 by Plaid Enterprises. Courtesy of Plaid Enterprises, Inc.*

*Add individual or central motifs last. From Stenciling Your Walls by Jane Gauss, copyright © 1990 by Plaid Enterprises. Courtesy of Plaid Enterprises, Inc.*

This primitive-style bedroom is an excellent example of how to combine horizontal, vertical, and central motifs. Starting with the colors of the patchwork quilt, which provided the only source of color in the room, a deep blue was added to create a pleasing country look. The stenciling doesn't detract from the antiques, which remain the focal point of the room's decor. Designed and stenciled by Jane Gauss for Plaid Enterprises. From The Complete Book of Wall Stenciling by Jane Gauss, copyright © 1984 by Plaid Enterprises. Courtesy of Plaid Enterprises, Inc.

This detail of a tiny laundry room illustrates how an effective use of color and design can convert a utilitarian space into a showplace. The ceiling, soffit, and the bottom half of the walls to chair rail height were painted in a slightly darker value of the light cream wall color. The tree motif, which was adapted from the border, was enlarged and centered on the painted wall cabinets. The stenciling on the ceiling makes the room appear larger, leaving the light, uncluttered wall areas available for the laundry equipment. Designed and stenciled by Jane Gauss for Plaid Enterprises. From The Complete Book of Wall Stenciling by Jane Gauss, copyright © 1984 by Plaid Enterprises. Courtesy of Plaid Enterprises, Inc.

# PREPARING WALLS FOR STENCILING

The general rule for surface preparation for stenciling applies to walls, too: Virtually any surface can be stenciled as long as it doesn't have a high gloss or sheen. Below are some parameters for preparing and protecting a range of wall surfaces for stenciling.

## PLASTER AND DRYWALL

Paint plaster or drywall surfaces with a flat or satin-finish paint, either oil- or latex-based. With most paints, a minimum of two coats is required for an even finish. Allow paint to cure for at least 24 hours before stenciling.

Semi-gloss paint is generally not recommended as a base for stenciling paints, especially stick paints and japan paints, as its finish interferes with the quality of a stencil print and prevents the stenciling paint from curing completely. In an area such as a bathroom or kitchen, however, it would be impractical to leave walls with a flat, unwashable finish. In these instances, or if you've stenciled in a high-traffic area, you will want to preserve your prints with a protective coating. (See "Protecting High-Traffic Areas," below.) In any event, be sure to save at least a small amount of paint for touch-ups or correcting mistakes.

## TEXTURED WALLS

Textured walls need not remain unstenciled. In fact, depending on the stenciling technique, the surface texture of a wall can enhance natural color variations in a stenciled print. For example, block printing and applying stencil crayons with a brush both work well with textured walls.

Bear in mind that the degree of texture will affect your choice of stencil design. In general, an open, flowing design is more flattering for a textured wall. If a design features tiny motifs, the texture of the wall might disrupt the continuity of the print. Test the design on a small, concealed area that can be easily painted over—behind a door, for example—before tackling an entire room.

## WALLPAPER

If you'd like to stencil a wallpapered room but are less than enthusiastic about the prospect of a messy renovation, you may want to consider leaving the wallpaper in place and stenciling directly over it. As with painted surfaces, stenciling paints adhere most effectively to matte finishes.

- *If the room is papered in a solid color or mini-print,* stenciling can provide a decorator touch by blending with the wallpaper's color and/or design.
- *If you're stenciling in an older home* whose walls were initially papered to cover cracks and faults in the plaster, there is no need to remove the paper before stenciling. Check to see that all seams are glued, then reattach any loose sections to the walls. Paint the wallpaper with a flat or satin-finish oil-based paint or a primer specifically designed to cover wallpaper. (A water-based latex paint might dissolve the surface of the wallpaper.) It is recommended that you apply at least two coats of paint to sufficiently cover all patterns or colors that may show through.

## WOOD OR PLYWOOD PANELING

Before stenciling a paneled room, it is recommended that you work on a sample piece of paneling first by preparing its surface, stenciling it, then applying any finish coats. This is the best way to verify whether the end results are what you had originally anticipated, and to make any adjustments for the actual project.

- *If you're working on unfinished wood,* apply a base stain or clear wood sealer.
- *If you're working on prefinished paneling,* wash it first to remove wax or dirt. If the paneling is stained dark, test translucent paints on a small sample to see whether the stain obscures their colors. In such a case, you might want to reevaluate your color choices, or try stenciling your motifs first in white acrylic, then stenciling your colors over it. The white will radiate through translucent colors, allowing them to stand out against a dark background. This technique will work on any dark background.
- *If your paneling has a "factory" gloss finish,* paint may not adhere to its surface. You can either (1) paint the paneling with an oil-based flat or satin-finish paint, or (2) apply a flat varnish before stenciling, then apply another coat of varnish (satin or gloss) to the entire surface to restore its sheen after the stenciling has dried completely.
- *After stenciling,* wait at least three days before applying the finish coats of varnish or polyurethane. Test a small section before applying polyurethane or urethane. Note that oil-based polyurethanes can yellow with age.

## PROTECTING HIGH-TRAFFIC AREAS

For most rooms, stenciling doesn't require a protective finish. The stenciled portion of any wall is as washable as the background paint. There are some areas, however, that require a semi-gloss scrubbability.

The scrubbability of flat or eggshell-finish paint in a kitchen area, for example, where there is frequent splashing around the sink or spattering grease from the stove, would be limited. Stenciling in kitchens, bathrooms, laundry or mud rooms, and children's room usually need the protection of a finish coat. This protection can be achieved very easily with several quality products in a variety of surface finishes, available from your local paint store.

- *If the background surface is very light,* select a water-based clear urethane. Oil-based finishes yellow over time.
- *Apply the protective finish with a flat roller.* Most products dry very quickly. If the finish appears to be streaked once it's dried, then you need to apply a second coat.
- *To repaint a varnished or finished wall,* treat it as if it were painted with a semi-gloss paint. To repaint, either lightly sand the wall or apply a primer coat.
- *You can apply a protective coating any time after stenciling.* Even if the room in question doesn't fall into one of those categories that generally requires a protective finish, it might receive more wear and tear than you originally expected. Simply wash off dirt or fingerprints with a mild wall cleaner, then apply the finish coat.

# MEASURING AND LAYING OUT BORDERS

Once you've prepared your walls, gathered all your supplies, and made several paper proofs as guides for color and placement, you're ready to start stenciling—definitely the easiest and most enjoyable part of the process.

But where do you start? That depends on the size of your design's *repeat,* which is a single grouping of design motifs. The two categories of border designs are based on this measurement.

- *Continuous flowing borders,* such as a vine with berries or flowers. The repeats of these borders usually measure 8 inches or less.
- *Centered borders* are those that feature a prominent design element, such as a large swag or a cluster of flowers. The repeats of these borders usually measure more than 8 inches.

Measure the repeat of your stencil design, then follow the instructions below that pertain to the particular type of border. If you're stenciling a room whose walls are all at least 10 feet long, follow the stenciling instructions for a continuous flowing border regardless of the stencil's repeat measurement. Your paper proofs will prove to be invaluable measuring tools for determining the amount of stretching or squeezing required for each repeat.

Use only light-colored chalk to mark your walls. To remove chalk marks, use an artist's eraser. A graphite pencil mark can't be removed completely from a painted surface, and pencil erasers can leave permanent red smudges.

## CONTINUOUS FLOWING BORDERS

Note that the guidelines for stenciling a continuous flowing border are the same as those for hanging wallpaper.

1. Locate the dominant corner of the room, which is the first one you see as you walk in. You'll begin stenciling at this corner, move in both directions, and end in the subordinate corner, which is usually somewhere near the doorway.
2. Starting in the dominant corner and, moving to either the left or the right, stencil approximately two-thirds of the wall. Then, using a paper proof, determine how the design will fit into the next corner. For example, if your paper proof indicates that one of the stencil's primary motifs will fall directly into the corner, you should either *stretch* or *squeeze* each repeat consistently by 1/4 to 1/2 inch as you stencil the final third of the wall to prevent an awkward corner break.
3. After stenciling the first wall and completing the corner where the first and second walls meet, continue stenciling the second wall. If the second wall is one that meets the subordinate corner, stencil only two-thirds of its length.
4. Return to the dominant corner and continue stenciling in the other direction. As you stencil toward the corner where the third and fourth walls meet, use the paper proof again to determine whether it's necessary to stretch or squeeze the motifs. If this corner is the subordinate one, stencil only two-thirds of the third wall's length.
5. On the two walls that meet in the subordinate corner, use paper proof to mark how the design will end. By either stretching or squeezing the design repeat on each of these walls, you can match the design perfectly. If there is a small space remaining, select a nondescript part of the design (such as a small sprig of leaves) and use it to finish the repeat, rather than ending with part of a prominent motif.

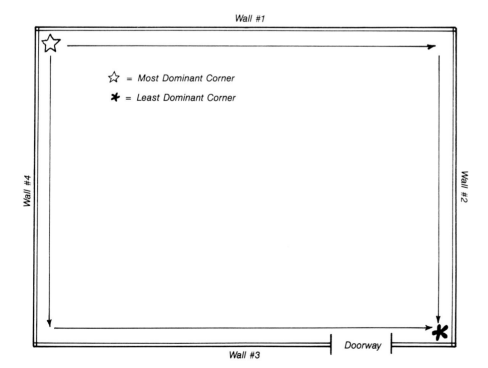

Wall #1

☆ = Most Dominant Corner

✱ = Least Dominant Corner

Wall #4

Wall #2

Wall #3

Doorway

*When stenciling a continuous flowing border, begin with the dominant corner of the room and work in both directions toward the subordinate corner. From Stenciling Your Walls by Jane Gauss, copyright © 1990 by Plaid Enterprises. Courtesy of Plaid Enterprises, Inc.*

## HANDLING CORNERS

Although you can prevent large or prominent motifs from falling into or on corners by stretching or squeezing repeats, with a continuous flowing border, parts of the design will inevitably traverse corners. A stencil print should fade almost imperceptibly into or over a corner while maintaining the basic flow of the design.

1. Attach the stencil to the wall with tape, leaving the portion of the stencil free that will continue onto the next wall.
2. Using a feathering motion or a light sweeping stroke, apply the paint into or on the corner. This is the only instance where a fade-out of color is acceptable.
3. Attach the remaining portion of the stencil to the adjoining wall, then detach the stencil from the first wall. Stencil this portion, feathering the design from the corner onto the adjacent wall.

Do not try to bend the stencil and dab paint into or around a corner. Your eye will immediately be drawn to this unusually strong accent of color. When the color is feathered to a gentle fade, your eye will naturally complete any shapes that are incomplete.

## CENTERED BORDERS

With this type of border, you'll start at the center of the wall with the center of the design and work toward the corners.

1. Measure the length of the repeat.
2. Find the center of each wall and mark it lightly with chalk.
3. Calculate the number of repeats that will fit onto each half wall. By starting at the center of the design and the center of the wall, the corners will work out the same. Remember that every design has at least two (or sometimes even three) motifs that can act as center points. If the one you selected doesn't fit well into the corners, remeasure the design using the other. In a swag design, for example, the center point can be either the actual center of the swag or the end of the swag. Use the center point that enables you to end or begin the corner with a complete motif.

4. Double check your calculations by placing the paper proof at the center of the wall and "walking" the design into the corner.
5. Rarely do the dimensions of walls and stencil repeats coordinate so that the corners work out perfectly. In most cases, you will need to stretch or squeeze the repeats to make them fit.

## VERTICALS

Stencil vertical borders only after all the horizontal borders in the room have been completed. Begin and end each vertical border 1/2 to 1 inch from a horizontal border.

### VERTICALS WITH GUIDELINES

A guideline for a vertical border is an existing architectural molding, such as a corner, window, door, or chair rail. Always stencil 1/2 to 3/4 inch from corners, and always work from top to bottom.

Before stenciling vertical borders, use a bubble level to check the plumb of the moldings. A border that follows the line of a molding will draw the eye to a crooked doorjamb or window frame. This is particularly important in older homes. Do not add stenciling to areas that will accentuate architectural problems. If the moldings and corners are plumb, use the bubble level and a piece of chalk to mark a parallel vertical line.

### VERTICALS WITHOUT GUIDELINES

Vertical guidelines without borders are used to divide a wall into sections or panels, or to add a striped effect to a wall. There are no set rules for determining how many verticals to use on a single wall. Attach a series of paper proofs to the wall and evaluate a few arrangements.

1. Once you've determined their number and placement, use a tape measure or yardstick to precisely measure the distance from the center of each vertical.
2. Use a bubble level to complete the guidelines by lightly marking with a piece of chalk. Align this line with the registration marks on the stencil.

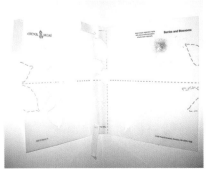

1. Affix the stencil to the wall with tape, leaving the portion that continues onto the adjoining wall free.

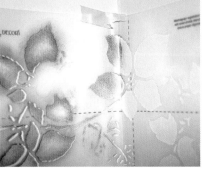

2. Use a feathering motion or a light sweeping stroke so that the color fades gradually into or on the corner.

3. A finished corner. Note how the area of diminished color appears visually complete. Blossoms and berries stencil from Plaid Enterprises.

## INDIVIDUAL OR CENTRAL MOTIFS

As with horizontal and vertical borders, use paper proofs to determine the placement and spacing for central motifs. Whether the motifs are the same or different will affect their placement and spatial relationships. Do not use central motifs where they would be partially covered by wall groupings or picture frames.

### IDENTICAL CENTRAL MOTIFS

The placement for central motifs that are all the same is determined by measuring the *positive space,* which means that the space *from the center of one motif to the center of the next* should be the same.

1. Tape your paper proofs in position on the wall to determine an approximate layout.
2. Measure the distance from the bottom of the frieze or ceiling line to the top of the chair rail or kickplate. This is the amount of positive space available for the central motifs.
3. Divide this amount by one more than the number of designs you want to stencil in that space. The result is the amount of space you will leave between motifs. For example, if there is 6 feet (72 inches) between the bottom of the frieze to the top of the kickplate, and you want to stencil three motifs within that space, divide 72 by 4. This calculation allows for 18 inches between the centers of the motifs.

4. Begin measuring from the bottom of the frieze or ceiling line. Make a light chalk mark to indicate the center point for the first motif.
5. Measure the same distance from the center point. Make another mark to indicate the center of the second motif.
6. Continue measuring and marking in the same manner until you've marked the center of the last motif.

### DISSIMILAR CENTRAL MOTIFS

The measurement for central motifs that are dissimilar uses the available *negative space,* which means that the space *between* motifs should be the same.

1. Position your paper proofs in an approximate layout.
2. Measure the total space availabe for the central motifs.
3. Measure the height of each motif in a specific row. Subtract the sum of their heights (the total space required for stenciling) from the available space. The remaining amount is the measurement that will be used as the space between motifs.
4. You will need one segment of space more than the number of motifs because you'll need to leave space above and below as well as between them. For example, if the available space is 6 feet (72 inches) and the sum of the heights of three motifs is 28 inches, subtract 28 from 72, then divide by 4 (one more than the number of motifs). This calculation allows for 11 inches above, below, and between motifs.

*For a centered border, use the center point that enables you to begin and end at each corner with a complete motif. From* Stenciling Your Walls *by Jane Gauss, copyright © 1990 by Plaid Enterprises. Courtesy of Plaid Enterprises, Inc.*

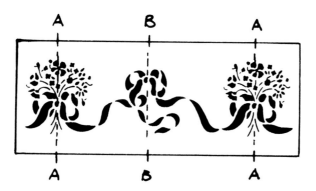

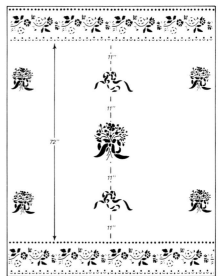

To determine the amount of space to leave between dissimilar central motifs, subtract the sum of the heights of the motifs from the available space, then divide by the number of motifs plus one. From Stenciling Your Walls by Jane Gauss, copyright © 1990 by Plaid Enterprises. Courtesy of Plaid Enterprises, Inc.

*To measure spacing for identical central motifs, divide the available space by the number of motifs you're planning to stencil plus one. From* Stenciling Your Walls *by Jane Gauss, copyright © 1990 by Plaid Enterprises. Courtesy of Plaid Enterprises, Inc.*

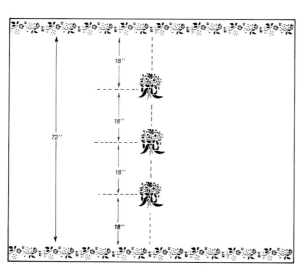

# ACCENT BORDERS

A border doesn't necessarily have to be stenciled all the way around a room. You can use a *partial* or *accent border* to highlight one specific area or establish subtle visual connections to create a complete decor. Martha Johnson designed an accent border featuring lilacs and butterflies to accentuate her living room's large windows. In this particular project, the surface preparation, which involved removing wallpaper, refurbishing the plaster walls, and glazing the walls in several layers of translucent, gradated color, comprised the bulk of the work.

After stripping the wallpaper and smoothing the walls with plaster, Martha primed and painted the walls and window frames with white semi-gloss latex paint and the baseboards with light violet alkyd satin enamel paint. She then mixed a light glaze consisting of 1 part of the alkyd satin enamel paint, 1 part glazing liquid, and 1 part mineral spirits (kerosene could also be used), increasing the ratio of paint to create two darker glazes. When working with strong paint solvents such as mineral spirits, make sure the room is adequately ventilated and wear a respirator.

After taping the surrounding surfaces, Martha began painting the base of the wall with the darkest glaze. To prevent a hard edge from forming between colors, as Martha applied the darkest glaze a second person applied the medium-value glaze immediately afterward. As the glazes met and were blended by a large stipple paint brush, a gradual transition from one color to the next began to emerge. After all three glazes were applied, Martha worked a stipple brush over the entire wall, across the top, from side to side, up and down, softening its color with each pass of the brush.

Martha stenciled the lilacs in a range of colors, including medium pink, white, mauve, and crimson, adding dimension by handpainting some of the background petals with a liner brush. She created highlights and dark tones in the leaves by mixing green with both dark blue and yellow and using a mask to produce veins and shading. Using a liner brush and black stencil crayon thinned with turpentine, Martha also handpainted the legs, antennae, and wing veins of the tiger swallowtails.

1. The areas surrounding the walls were taped, then glazed in three sections.

2. Stenciling the first overlay. Masks were used to produce veins and shading in the leaves.

3. Adding depth within the flowers using a liner brush and crimson thinned with turpentine.

52

4. Each accent border is centered over a window, with blooms cascading down the sides of its frame. The butterflies appear both in flight and at rest on flowers. Designed and stenciled by Martha Johnson.

# BORDER STYLES

A border is where many novice stencilers begin practicing their craft. There are hundreds of beginner-level border stencils on the market that are both affordable and easy-to-use, but don't stop there in your search for the "perfect" design. Look at the many examples on the next few pages and let them spark some new ideas. Then sit in the middle of the room you're planning to decorate and envision which designs and treatments might work for you.

*This graceful Victorian design was inspired by a lace collar. The stencil was positioned approximately 12 inches below the ceiling line so that the windows and door moldings would create visual breaks. Acrylic paints in several values were used to create delicate shadings with sharp, crisp edges. Designed and stenciled by Mary Severns.*

*The free-flowing pattern of this stencil design transforms this living room atrium into an English country garden. A stipple stroke was used to achieve an optical mix of colors in both the leaves and the flowers. Details were added after the stencils were removed, enhancing the freehand look of the work. Stencils designed by Jan Dressler; stenciled by Dawne Marie Johnson.*

*Stenciled with oil-based opaque semi-gloss interior housepaint over a semi-gloss surface, these randomly placed cows simultaneously echo and counter the checkerboard of tiles in this charming bathroom. The "pasture" was added later with a separate grass stencil. Designed and stenciled by Ann Hooe.*

*In this child's bedroom, a continuous rope border and an "ocean" applied with sea sponges are the key elements in an amusing marine fantasy. The seahorse is also featured as an accent in an arrangement of throw pillows, whose colors match those used in the wall motifs. Underwater Sea Adventure Home Decorating Kit and Video by Bunny DeLorie and Kathy Curtis of FeFiFaux Finish.*

*This attractive accent border for the kitchen was inspired by the stenciler's dinnerware. After making a photocopy of a dinner plate, she isolated specific design elements and laid them out in a repeat. The lightly textured walls were painted in latex enamel, then sanded with extra-fine sandpaper to improve bonding with the acrylic stencil paints. While no special sealer was required for the motifs above the cabinets, the stencil over the stove was protected with water-based varnish. Designed and stenciled by Jan Demerath.*

The winding trail of this block-printed ivy border makes the cove molding look like it's suspended in midair. The molding, which can also be used as a plate rail, was attached directly to the wall about 12 inches below the ceiling line. A line of ¼-inch masking tape was used to guide the general flow of the design, with a second line of tape used for the intertwining leaves. For complete instructions on block printing, see page 39. Designed and block-printed by Vi and Stu Cutbill.

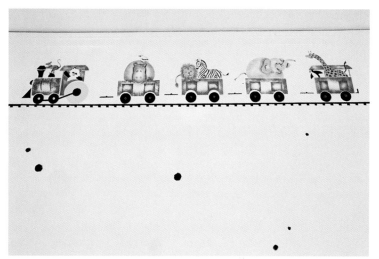

A baby's birth announcement was the inspiration for this whimsical design. The train track was stenciled first in order to establish a visual reference point. The cars were then stenciled with two interchangeable overlays, which were used to modify the design in different areas of the room. The animals were then stenciled and their features painted by hand. As a finishing touch, irregularly shaped dots inspired by the layette fabric were randomly stenciled in black. Designed and stenciled by Peggy Eisenberg.

This stenciler used the proportions of an octagonal bathroom window as the basis for a graceful trellis design. The neutral green of the trellis provides a subtle backdrop for the randomly placed vines, flowers, and berries, which were stenciled with a light touch. Designed and stenciled by Ann Hooe.

The unusual placement of accent floral and bird motifs transformed this small guest room into an enjoyable retreat. In addition to displaying other room accessories, the shelves provide a venue for an example of the stacking technique (see page 36), as can be seen in the vine and parrots (shown above). Note how the texture of the wall enhances the dimensional look of the prints. Designed and stenciled by Mary Severns.

This nursery border was stenciled on a white stripe painted over a soft blue wall. Placing a border at crib height prevents it from being interrupted by the crib itself and allows the baby to enjoy its design and colors, too. While a chair rail is usually 30 to 36 inches off the floor, a crib rail looks best at 48 inches or more off the floor. Designed and stenciled by Julia Hierl Burmesch.

Fruit and vegetable swags stenciled over a sponged background of gray and beige lend warmth to this white contemporary kitchen. The stencils were initially set in with acrylics, then overpainted in oils by hand. Designed and stenciled by Heather Whitehouse.

*This colorful pheasant frieze was stenciled over a black background to create maximum contrast. Stenciled by Jo Miller.*

*A stenciled plate rail displaying several artfully arranged volumes provides an unusual doorway accent. Designed and stenciled by Toni Grove.*

*Adapted from a beautiful vanity sink by Kohler, an ivy frieze and an accent border of peonies lend charming touches to this small powder room. Peony stencil designed by Jeanette McKibben; ivy stencil designed by Chris Smith; stenciled by Chris Smith.*

The owner of this house wanted to bring light and life to an otherwise dark and drab living/dining room. The walls of the dining room were first painted bright white, and the ceiling above the soffit was painted in a pale sky blue, then sponged with flat white latex paint to create a subtle cloud effect. Three of the living room walls were painted a soft, buttery yellow. The remaining wall, which separates the two rooms and contains an archway, was first painted white, then stenciled in an all-over basketweave (complete with braided trim), using yellow paint that had been thinned slightly to make it easier to work with. The basketweave provided the perfect backdrop for the freeform floral prints, which seem to be entangled in it.

The stencils were taken from sets that include a variety of flower, leaf, basket, and trellis designs, which gives the stenciler the freedom to create one-of-a-kind prints. The flowers and leaves were stenciled with brushes and acrylic paints in a wide range of colors. The paints were thinned with extender to achieve a smooth, creamy consistency, making them easier to work with when using the smaller brushes to create three-dimensional effects in the flowers and leaves. In the dining room, a grapevine trellis was stenciled around the soffit with smaller flowers in random groupings, some of which appeared to wrap around the edge of the soffit trellis and extend toward the ceiling sky. After the stenciling was completed, leaf veins and meandering vines and tendrils were added using thinned paint and liner brushes. Stencils from the Stencils and Strokes Collection by Melanie Royals; designed and stenciled by Melanie Royals.

# STENCILING A CEILING

Don't discount your ceiling as a surface for stenciling. As shown by Sherry Gholson, a ceiling can be as effective as a wall for displaying stenciling that complements every aspect of an established decor. Sherry divided her ceiling into a grid that reflects both the structure of the room and the elements of its decor, then used the grid as a part of her design.

Working on a smooth drywall surface painted with a soft mauve latex paint, Sherry stenciled an arbor of crisscrossing twigs by following a chalked grid that ensured a balanced distribution of prints. She then stenciled wisteria blossoms in a freeform manner, varying the direction and orientation of the stencil so that a repeat couldn't be discerned.

There are a few logistical issues to take into consideration, not the least of which are getting at the ceiling in the first place and the physical demands of looking *up* at your work. First, you'll need a walking scaffold. For a standard 8-foot ceiling, you can either purchase one of the new ladders that can be configured into a scaffold, or you can make a scaffold by positioning two 2 × 6s between two stepladders. For very high or vaulted ceilings, you'll need to rent a real scaffold. Instead of tape, use repositionable spray adhesive to keep stencils flush to the ceiling. If the grid of your design is fairly simple and the prospect of climbing on a scaffold dampens your enthusiasm, consider working on paintable ceiling wallpaper and installing it later.

Sherry also has a few helpful hints for stenciling a ceiling with liquid paints: Keep two small bottles on your paint tray, one filled with background color for quick touch-ups, the other filled with solvent. In addition to using the solvent to freshen paints, you can rejuvenate your applicators without getting off the ladder.

## LAYING OUT A CEILING

The following are some general guidelines for dividing a ceiling into sections. Note that these can also be used to plan a gridded floor pattern. (See "Stenciled Floors," page 68.)

1. Measure the dimensions of the room, taking into account all its structural features. Then draw its floor plan on graph paper, using a scale of 1 square = 6 inches (or 2 squares to 1 foot), indicating the position of the major elements of the decor, such as light fixtures and large pieces of furniture.

2. When determining how the stenciling should be distributed within the grid, carefully review the floor plan to decide where the stenciling should *not* appear, as well as where you would like to add areas of interest.

3. Sketch several grid possibilities, making sure that its segments are generous and correspond to the dimensions of the room. When gridding any surface, note that an odd number of segments usually creates a more pleasing effect than an even number.

4. Using a light-colored chalk pencil or a chalk line whose chalk box has been filled with a light-colored chalk mixture, mark the ceiling with the grid lines. Use the grid to guide your stenciling, removing each segment as you complete it.

*Sherry Gholson's room grid includes structural elements as well as major decorative components such as a baby grand piano and the central ceiling fixture.*

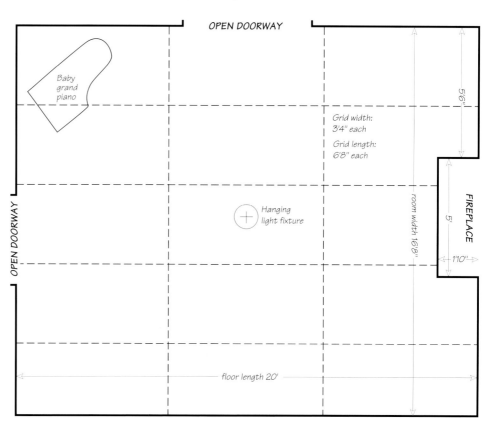

*The twig arbor was stenciled over the chalk lines of the grid. Twigs in Arbor stencil designed by Jan Dressler.*

*To emphasize certain areas, wisteria blossoms were also stenciled on the wall. In this example, a chickadee is the featured accent. Wisteria stencil designed by Deb Mores.*

*The rectangular segments of the grid correspond to the flow of the room.*

*Although the fireplace is not centered on the wall, it remains the focal point because the ceiling is now divided into an odd number of segments. Designed and stenciled by Sherry Gholson.*

# CEILING GALLERY

As you can see from the imaginative treatments on these two pages, there's more than one way to stencil a ceiling. A grid may be useful for organizing a ceiling composition, but who's to say that a ceiling grid must be rigid or methodical? Even if walls are papered, a ceiling offers blank canvas for decorative possibilities. Skies, both day and night, are natural—and popular—ceiling motifs. Techniques can run the gamut, from stenciling on canvas panels to sponged color to airbrush. Use the examples shown here as a starting point for your own designs.

*In this unusual tapestry-theme project, strips of canvas 42 inches wide by 16 feet long were primed, stenciled, and varnished, then installed by a professional wallpaper hanger to an exposed-beam ceiling. The design, which required twelve stencils, nine colors of japan paint, and two weeks of labor to complete, was adapted from a scrap of fabric. Designed and stenciled by Anne Rullman and Lynn Terrel.*

*An elegant coffered ceiling is transformed into a series of skylights that open to a perpetual nighttime sky. The recessed panels were painted with a midnight blue latex paint, then an even darker blue glaze was sponged on to give the surface movement and depth. Stars in several sizes were stenciled with gold leaf. Designed and stenciled by Anne Rullman and Lynn Terrel.*

The Victorian lighting fixture at the center of this bedroom ceiling provided the inspiration for a circular stencil motif of bells and ribbons in sage and mauve. To draw a precise circle, drill a hole at each end in a piece of wood cut to the desired radius, attach one end to the center of the circle by inserting a nail through the hole, then insert a pencil through the other and use it to draw the circumference of the circle. The lattice stencil was handcut and adjusted to fill the remaining ceiling to the corners. Stencils from Stencil Decor® by Plaid Enterprises; ceiling designed and stenciled by Jo Miller.

This oak leaf and pine cone border trimmed in gold was designed to accent an antique ceiling medallion. Designed and stenciled by Jo Miller.

A lattice overlooking a cloud-filled sky is the theme for this kitchen ceiling. The technique is very simple: A lattice stencil over a white background leaves the lattice white as the sky behind is stenciled, in this example, with light blue eggshell-finish interior latex paint and a foam roller. The lattice stencil was left in place when stenciling the foliage and blossoms so that they would appear to be growing from behind it. The lattice stencil was then removed, and the foreground foliage was added with a single wisteria branch stencil used again and again—overlapped, rotated, and flopped—with each layer of leaves in a slightly different color. The ceiling was then finished in light blue, leaving cloud areas white. Lattice stencil from Buckingham Stencils Garden Room Collection; designed and stenciled by Sandra Buckingham.

The vaulted ceiling in this dramatic entryway (above) is graced by playful cupids delicately shaded with airbrush. (For more information on airbrush techniques, see "Stenciling with Airbrush," page 106.) Designed and stenciled by Sheri Hoeger.

# THE STENCILED ENVIRONMENT

Over the past few years, many stencilers have begun to use their craft to produce elaborately detailed environments. These innovators have transcended traditional stenciling treatments that exclusively employ coordinated vertical and horizontal borders to create fully illustrated themes, either natural, fanciful, or architectural (or a combination of these). A by-product of this trend is a renewed and avid interest in trompe l'oeil (see page 114), in which stenciling and a host of other decorative painting techniques are used to engage the viewer by challenging his or her perception of reality.

In the examples shown below and on the next three pages, the stencilers have used a variety of techniques and decorating approaches. (Although all of the projects are children's rooms, they are certainly not the only venue for such treatment.) These projects are misleading in their complexity, as all of their techniques are well within the ambitious beginner's grasp and differ from the projects shown earlier in this chapter only in the extent to which stenciling was used as an element of the decor. What sets these kinds of projects apart from others is the time, patience, and commitment they require.

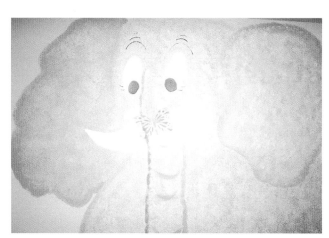

*Cheerful yellow walls provide the backdrop for these jungle animal motifs, which were executed largely by hand due to the size of the forms. An effort was made to integrate the images with the structural elements of the room, as the giraffe rests his head atop the window frame while feeding on a leaf and the zebra remains partially hidden "behind" a door. Using chalk outlines as a guide, kraft paper cut into curved masks helped maintain the outside edges of the shapes during the painting process. These masks were particularly useful in rendering the zebra's stripes. Acrylic paints were sponged on with natural sea sponges, and details such as eyes and eyebrows were added by hand. The butterfly alighting on the elephant's nose was stenciled separately. Designed and stenciled by Christina Gibson.*

Part of this small child's bedroom was partitioned off with a wall, into which were cut a child-sized door and window openings to create an indoor playhouse. To complete the illusion, the facade of a child-sized cottage was painted on the wall, incorporating the window and door. The remaining wall space was stenciled to resemble a fenced garden.

(Left) The walls were brushed with washes of diluted household latex paint, starting with blue at the ceiling, blending into lilac and finally pink at the bottom of the wall. When the wall was thoroughly dry, it was brushed again with a series of transparent glazes, from blue at the top to rose at the bottom. The pickets were stenciled one at a time, using a foam roller and white latex paint. (It usually takes two or three coats to stencil a solid white, since such a small amount of paint is used each time.) Shadows were added with stencils and pale transparent

gray paint. For the garden plants, a few simple stencils were used repeatedly to build up bushes or trees. The pickets were protected with masks as the foliage behind them was stenciled, then the masks were removed and the foreground plants were added in stronger colors. (Right) A watchful cat surveys the garden from her perch in the cottage window. Stencils from the Buckingham Stencils Garden Room Collection by Sandra Buckingham; designed and stenciled by Sandra Buckingham.

In this medieval fantasy children's bedroom, a dragon climbs over a castle wall to find a playmate. After the sky and clouds were sponged on in two tones of sky blue and white, the outlines of the castle parapet and the dragon were masked off with kraft paper. The individual rocks in the castle wall were defined by lines of masking tape, which were also used to create the mortar between them. The dragon was painted with

both bristle brushes (for outlines) and sponge applicators (for large areas), with shading and texture added by sponging on a second shade of green. Cellulose household sponges were cut into various shapes, daubed in paint, and pressed on to create polka dots. Facial details were added with artist's brushes. The various plants and insects provide an interesting contrast to the large shapes of the dragon and castle.

An idea that was reworked several times during the project was the addition of the children's names somewhere on the walls. Eventually, the stenciler decided to paint a castle window between the two beds, over which a "banner" would be hung. The sky and stone were masked and sponged in, then the banner was added by applying paint with a sponge applicator through a large stencil of craft paper. The names were drawn on a second kraft paper stencil, with a sponge applicator, cut with a utility knife, stenciled in blue and violet. A few bugs were added for interest and continuity. Designed and stenciled by Catherine A. Stone.

This charming detail creates a visual link between the two windows and their actual vista.

Bunnies, bears, and a nursery rhyme frieze in oversized type all contribute to create an impressive nursery wonderland. The nursery rhyme frieze was executed with a set of alphabet stencils: "Once upon a time, there was a little girl named Molly Clare who played tag-a-long with bunny and bear." Stencils designed by Andreae Designs; stenciled by Marjorie Andreae and Julie Robinson. Photographs copyright © Jay Asquini, Asquini, Inc., 1994.

After the characters were stenciled, a second chalk line was drawn 11 inches from the chair rail as a guideline for the large accent pieces such as trees, fences, and bushes. Rows of grass and flowers were added at the first two chalk lines as well as at a third drawn 2 inches above the chair rail. The sun, birds, and clouds were then added at various levels. Mylar cutouts were used over several motifs to add depth and dimension to the scene.

The character stencils were taped to the walls in various locations to determine placement, then a chalk line 4 inches above the chair rail was drawn to keep them in alignment. To block out the underlying pink wall color, each stencil was basecoated with white using a small sponge. Both swirling and stippling techniques were used to apply the paint colors using a very dry brush: Swirling strokes were used on some of the animals to create the illusion of fur, while stippling was used to create shadows on the fence and lend solidity to small areas.

# STENCILED FLOORS

Frequently left unadorned or hidden beneath wall-to-wall carpeting, floors are a sadly undervalued commodity in contemporary home decor. For the stenciler, a floor presents yet another opportunity to decorate, beautify, and personalize a room.

Starting with the colonial era, the history of stenciled floors in the United States offers a survey of decorative painting techniques, from graining and faux finishing to spattering and marquetry. As with wallcovering, the cost of carpeting at that time was prohibitive even for the wealthy, since it could only be imported from Europe. As a result, painted and stenciled floors could be found in many elegant homes and inns, particularly in the northeastern United States, though due to continuing renovations, very few of these floors exist today.

In an article that appeared in the April, 1931 issue of *Magazine Antiques*, Esther S.F. Brazer states that "paint, as an interior finish, appears to have come into use in the colonies about 1725. Before that date its advantages as a preservative may not have been recognized; or . . . the scarcity of pigments and oils in this country may have prevented its employment." Pumpkin yellow was a popular floor color, since it simulated to some extent the color of a wood floor. Indian red, gray, and brown were also prevalent. After floors were first painted, it didn't take long for homeowners and itinerant decorators to use these surfaces for stenciling.

In the February, 1994 issue of *Early American Life,* an article by Jean Cresnic, "In Search of Old Painted Floors," shows a floor painted freehand, a style of decoration believed to be very early and rare, and most probably a precursor of stenciled flooring. Also accompanying Cresnic's

article is a photograph of a painted floor from the parlor of the Thomas Dodge House that dates from 1815. Although it was unsigned, it is attributed to Rufus Porter because its motifs are characteristic of his style and he is known to have worked in the area at the time. This floor was the stimulus for Linda Lefko's stenciled and handpainted wood floor (below left). The examples of stenciled floors shown on these two pages will motivate you to consider this routinely neglected surface as a means for expressing your creativity.

The decorative possibilities are virtually limitless. You'll find that inspiration will come from a variety of sources, and that your stenciling decisions will be based on a range of decorating needs. You can stencil a floor with a border that matches or complements a stenciled wall, transform utilitarian flooring into a definitive decorative element with a faux finish, or create a runner of stenciled carpet on a flight of stairs.

Preparation requirements will vary, depending on the surface. In any event, remove all dirt and wax before you begin. Stain a new wood floor with an oil-based stain or clear sealer. When painting floors, use only flat oil-based paint. If a floor is varnished or has a glossy finish, sand it well, then sweep it clean and vacuum it to remove all dust and debris. If necessary, fill cracks with wood putty before painting. Remove your shoes and work in your socks while stenciling, as an unfinished painted floor scuffs easily.

Although most of the examples shown here feature free-flowing designs, you can also stencil a floor with a gridded, all-over pattern. Simply adapt the instructions for "Laying Out a Ceiling" (see page 60) so that they work for your particular room.

*The primitive-style nautical motifs of this stenciled bathroom floor were derived from the view of the small lake on which the house is situated. To produce a color suggestive of colonial-style pumpkin pine, the pine floor was sanded smooth and coated with a 1:1 mixture of amber and clear shellac. The stenciling and painting were done directly on the shellac coat with acrylic paints. The border mural was painted predominantly freehand, while the coarse, arced brush strokes, which were adapted from the painted parlor floor at Thomas Dodge House, were stenciled. After the decoration had cured, five coats of water-based varnish were applied (three coats of gloss finish followed by two coats of satin finish). Water-based varnishes are nonyellowing, have no odor, and usually dry within 2 hours. Designed and stenciled by Linda Carter Lefko.*

*The colors of this delicately shaded autumn harvest floor were applied with an airbrush. Before stenciling, the floor was sealed with a clear sealer, then lightly sanded. The semi-transparent application of the motifs allows the grain of the wood to remain visible. (For more information on airbrush, see "Stenciling with Airbrush," page 106.) Designed and stenciled by Sheri Hoeger.*

*This kitchen floor was finished with white pickling, then stenciled with a free-flowing flower, ribbon, and vine design. The design was first laid out on paper proofs, then transferred to the floor. Three coats of polyurethane were added by a professional floor finisher after the stenciling had cured. Designed and stenciled by P. J. Tetreault.*

*Working over an existing finish of oil-based interior wall paint, the concrete floor of this sunroom was first sanded, then painted with one coat of gray oil-based industrial floor enamel. The floor was sanded with fine sandpaper to improve paint adhesion. The tile stencil, which consisted of four 6-inch squares, was sponged with dark cream, muted green, and red, all of which were loaded on the sponge simultaneously. Each tile was painted separately, shading from light in the center to dark around the edges, and the edges were stippled with dark brown floor paint to create depth. The diamond-shaped inset tiles were stenciled with cobalt blue. The floor was allowed to dry for one week, carefully vacuumed, then sponged with three heavy coats of acrylic floor polish, which allows concrete to breathe while protecting painted surfaces. Designed and stenciled by Linda Nelson Johnson and Lori Rohde.*

*To create a bold and dramatic decorative focal point, the motifs, patterns, and colors for this faux carpet (above) and runner (near left) were adapted from traditional Chinese carpeting. Prior to stenciling, the newly installed floor was sanded and sealed, then a circle 10 feet in diameter was drawn. The circle was divided into sectors, within which the positions of the stencils were marked with chalk. Each stencil motif consisted of three to four overlays and required some handpainted details. The black enamel background was carefully painted in after the stenciling was complete. The carpet was allowed to cure for two weeks before applying three coats of polyurethane. Designed and stenciled by Linda Durkin.*

*These stenciled flowerpots can add touches of color to a sunroom, patio, or deck. (For more information on stenciled accessories, both indoor and outdoor, see pages 93–95 and 103.) Courtesy of Plaid Enterprises, Inc.*

# OTHER STENCILING PROJECTS

The stenciler's approach to life is simple: "If it doesn't move, stencil it!" Before starting a project, you must take the necessary steps to make the intended surface receptive to paint and ensure your design's long life. In many instances, the physical characteristics or circumstances of a surface that might preclude stenciling can be dealt with through careful preparation and protective finishing.

In this chapter, stenciling is featured on a variety of surfaces, from furniture to fabrics, from ceramic tile to decorative accessories, as well as in the out-of-doors. In addition to the general information provided for each surface or material, the work of each stenciler is accompanied by invaluable project details specifying preparation as well as stenciling procedure.

# WOOD FURNITURE

Wood furniture offers a wide range of possible surface treatments and stenciling variations. Although many first-time stencilers are intimidated by its preparation requirements, even a beginner can obtain successful results with one of the many high-quality pieces of unfinished furniture available in a range of styles, from primitive to traditional to contemporary. If you're on a budget, think about giving that tired old piece in your attic or basement a new lease on life, or visit the flea markets and garage sales to look for a diamond in the rough. Use the examples shown through page 77 as inspiration, then seek out a local paint store where you can ask specific questions about products and preparation for your piece. If you need further assistance, you can call most of the major paint manufacturers direct. Their customer service representatives can give you valuable information on how to use their latest products.

Regardless of whether a piece of furniture is new or old, the one restriction for stenciling—that the surface cannot be slick or glossy—also applies here. Surface preparation for furniture may involve sanding, staining, glazing, and painting, but at the very least requires that all traces of wax and dirt be removed.

## STAINING

Stain should only be applied to raw wood, either new unfinished pieces or those that have been completely sanded and stripped. If an unfinished piece is rough, sand it first with a fine-grade sandpaper, then wipe it clean with a tack cloth. Some of the softer, more porous woods such as pine should then be brushed with a clear wood sealer (*not* a sanding sealer), which permits an even flow of stain in both color and absorption.

Be sure to stir the stain thoroughly and apply it according to the manufacturer's instructions, including drying times. Begin by proofing the stain on a small, concealed area of the piece, such as the inside of a drawer. If the stain raises the grain of the wood, sand the piece and wipe it clean with a tack cloth before staining, repeating this procedure if grain is raised after the first coat of stain. If the stain is too dark, wipe it with a clean piece of cheesecloth. If you don't like any of the ready-mixed stain colors, you can purchase natural stain and tint it with oil-based artist's pigments. For your first project, however, an oil-based penetrating stain that contains a sealer is your best choice.

After the piece has been stained and allowed to dry completely, it is ready for stenciling. If the wood is very porous, or if you're worried about damaging the stain with solvent while correcting a mistake, apply a coat of flat varnish to the stained surface. This prevents the paint from penetrating into the stain so that it can be easily removed.

## PAINTING

Begin by sanding the piece with fine to extra-fine sandpaper (always sand *with* the grain), then remove all dust with a tack cloth before painting. A painted base for stenciling can be either water- or oil-based, as long as its finish is flat rather than glossy. Apply paint with a good-quality brush to prevent streaky buildup.

If you're using an acrylic-based paint, which dries very rapidly, follow these easy steps:
1. Dampen a sponge brush slightly with water by wetting only the end of it, then blotting it on a paper towel.
2. Dip the moistened brush into a small amount of paint. Apply it to the surface quickly and evenly, covering a small section of the piece at a time.
3. Allow adequate drying time for the first coat, then buff lightly with a piece of brown paper bag. This "sanding" procedure is less likely to leave marks or remove paint. Wipe the entire piece with a tack cloth before applying the second coat. Let dry, then buff with paper again.
4. Repeat the procedure for the third coat. At least two and sometimes three coats are necessary to achieve a smooth, completely coated surface.

Some porous woods require additional drying time, especially around knotholes. These areas may show through the paint if not properly sealed first. Seal knotholes and woods like cedar and knotty pine completely with an alcohol-based primer. This flat, opaque white primer dries very quickly, then must be sanded before applying the first coat of paint.

## STENCILING STAINED OR PAINTED WOOD

After the stain or paint is completely dry, you're ready to stencil. You can use whichever paint you feel most comfortable working with, either liquid or solid. You can also use liquid and solid paints together, for example, by stenciling the first overlay with one type of paint and the next with another, but you should use the same type within each overlay. (Also, you can shade acrylics with creams or crayons, but not vice versa.) Remember that the surface texture and porosity of the wood will vary from piece to piece. It is essential that you use a *dry* brush and a *very light* initial circular motion to establish sharp edges.

Before finishing, allow the stencil prints to cure from one to five days, depending on the type of paint you've used.

## FINISHING

Since varnishes and polyurethanes vary in consistency, content, and finish (flat, satin, and high gloss), test the one you've purchased on a small area of the stenciling before you start. If there is any evidence that the finish is causing the stencil paint to blur or bleed, lightly mist the entire stenciled surface with a matte acrylic sealer. If the finish doesn't cause the paint to bleed, then you are ready to proceed with the entire piece. Always follow the manufacturer's instructions for application and drying times.

1. Wipe the entire piece with a tack cloth to remove all dust and lint.
2. Using a good-quality brush or applicator, apply the first coat of varnish with the grain, making sure that the finish doesn't run or puddle. A round bristle brush is excellent for rounded areas such as chair legs.
3. Allow the piece to dry completely in an area that is as free from dust as possible.
4. Before applying a second coat, wipe the entire piece with a tack cloth. Let dry completely.

   For a very fine, smooth finish, you can add the following steps:

1. After the second coat of finish is dry, sprinkle the piece with water and sand with an ultra-fine wet/dry sandpaper. Use a very light, even pressure so that none of the stencil print is removed. Wipe the entire piece with a tack cloth to remove dust and excess water.
2. Apply a third coat of finish and repeat the wet-sanding procedure. An additional one to two coats can be applied, depending on the depth of finish desired.
3. Following the final coat of finish and at least 12 to 18 hours of drying time, lightly buff the entire piece with #0000 steel wool. If desired, wax with a fine furniture wax, then tack off all residue.

*A bounty of stenciled fruit adapted from a wallpaper border has given this table-and-chair set a fresh new look. After stripping the pieces and spray painting them white, a groove was routed around the tabletop and the edge was painted brick red. The design was first stenciled with primer to provide it with an opaque, neutral surface, then stenciled with japan paints and a liner brush for color and depth. The stenciled edge was finished with two coats of water-based varnish. Designed and stenciled by Anne Rullman and Lynn Terrel.*

This lovely chest was refurbished to complement a bedroom decor. Dust and dirt were removed (along with all the drawer pulls), the peeling paint was sanded with medium-grit sandpaper, then the rest of the chest was smoothed with fine-grit sandpaper and wiped with a tack rag to remove residue. After sealing with a latex primer, the entire chest was painted with an off-white satin-finish paint. The delicate pearlescent glaze, which consisted of equal parts of paint, Floetrol (a paint additive), and water, was applied by lightly dabbing a small sea sponge over the surface, reloading only after the sponge was dry. The nine-overlay bridgeless stencil was designed to appear handpainted, when in fact only small details such as tendrils were painted with thinned solid paints and a liner brush. The chest was finished with two coats of nonyellowing acrylic varnish. Designed and stenciled by Linda M. Rogers.

An already finished piece can also reap the benefits of stenciling. This particular piece, painted with an off-white milkwood finish and trimmed in white and dark green, is further enhanced by the vines and potted topiary stenciled on its doors. The prints were finished with two coats of satin varnish. Clay pot stencil designed by Nancy Tribolet; vine and floral motifs designed by Christina Gibson; stenciled by Christina Gibson.

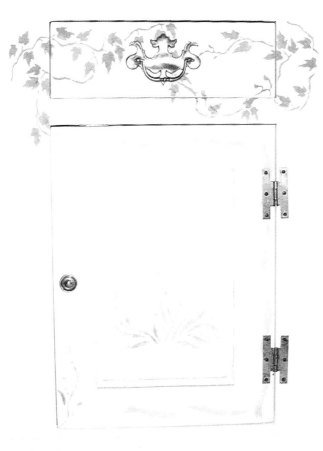

This pine hutch, which was originally finished in a dark stain, was painted, sponged, and stenciled in a complete makeover. After an initial sanding, tacking, and priming, the hutch was lightly sanded and tacked again, then painted with eggshell-finish white latex paint. Ribbons, ivy, and irises were stenciled in soft color with a sea sponge. The meandering vines lend a charming freeform look. Ivy and ribbon stencils designed by Jan Dressler; mountain wild iris stencil from Stencil Decor®; stenciled by Dawne Marie Johnson.

This previously unfinished armoire was painted and stenciled to create an old world effect. The piece was sanded, painted with latex satin enamel in a pale antique gold tone, then rag-rolled with an antique white oil glaze and trimmed in peach. The stencils were painted with acrylics, then antiqued with a spatter of soft gray oil glaze. The entire piece was finished with three coats of acrylic urethane. Stencils by DeeSigns Armoire collection; stenciled by Peggy Eisenberg.

A boy's bedroom becomes a southwestern showplace through a combination of stenciled walls and furniture. The armoire, originally a stained antique, was sanded thoroughly, then brushed with a heavy grayish white latex glaze that was then ragged off for an aged effect. The frieze and armoire trim were stenciled with the same pueblo-style design, and the mural on the doors was adapted from decorative fabrics. To achieve the bold, opaque prints that suggest the southwestern style, vibrant acrylic earth tones were pounced on with a stencil brush. The armoire was then varnished with three coats of latex urethane. Temple Steps stencil designed by Adele Bishop; mural designed and stenciled by Peggy Eisenberg.

(Above) The central panels in the doors of this prefinished entertainment center were lightly scuffed with extra-fine steel wool, then stenciled in acrylics with elegant freeform floral motifs. The panels were finished with two coats of matte-finish water-based varnish, polished with #0000 steel wool, and waxed. (Left) The original dark-toned finish of this antique silver chest looked severe against the floral-striped wallpaper that decorated the dining room. The chest was primed, painted, and then sponged in a complementary soft blue-gray. The multi-overlay stencil, which yielded delicate shading, was supplemented with freehand brushwork on the ribbons and bow and finished with one coat of matte-finish, water-based varnish. Designed and stenciled by P. J. Tetreault.

# FABRICS

Whether stenciled, block-printed, or painted freehand, fabrics have been colored and decorated with paints and dyes since civilization began. The earliest surviving fabric fragments are silks dating from the 6th century B.C. During the 16th century in Europe, stencils were used to apply flocking to fabrics for wall hangings.

Fabrics stenciled in the United States during the early 19th century show a high degree of skill in their execution. Many examples from this period, including intricate bedcovers and tablecloths, have survived to inspire generations of stenciling enthusiasts. These pieces were stenciled exclusively with oil-based paints, as they predated the development of fabric paints (formulated for use on fabrics and to endure repeated laundering) and acrylic paints (to which textile medium is added to produce colorfast prints). Some fabric paints can even withstand the chemicals used in dry cleaning. In any case, be sure to follow the manufacturer's instructions, and buy enough fabric so that you have an adequate surplus for proofing.

As most fabric paints must be heat-set with an iron or a hair dryer at a relatively high setting, natural fiber fabrics or 50/50 natural/synthetic blends are the best candidates for fabric painting. For example, various weights of cotton duck and pure silk are both wonderful painting surfaces, and can be treated with special dyes or finishing sprays to ensure colorfastness.

Stretch fabrics such as jersey and cotton knits can also be stenciled. To prevent distorted prints and keep the edges of the motifs crisp and sharp, simply pin the fabric to a board (do *not* stretch it tightly), or place a piece of very fine sandpaper beneath the fabric to keep it from sliding (this technique works well with other types of fabric, too). Very fine, sheer fabrics such as dotted Swiss are also suitable surfaces. Use a very dry brush with these fabrics, as too much paint will clog the weave. Although this makes the stenciling process more tedious, the end results are most rewarding.

Don't assume that a fabric must be white or light in color for stenciling to be visible. If you'd like to stencil a dark fabric, simply make your first print with white paint, let dry, then stencil the colors over it.

As shown through page 87, fabrics can be stenciled to complement and enhance a variety of decors. See how creative you can be by adding a touch of stenciling to fabrics. Remember that a blank piece of fabric carries the same decorative potential as a blank wall.

## STENCILING FABRICS

Many fabrics are treated with sizing during manufacturing to provide extra body. If sizing is left on the fabric, the paint will not penetrate as thoroughly, thus affecting its colorfastness. Before stenciling, wash your fabrics to remove sizing and prevent shrinkage or bleeding the first time you wash your stenciled item, then press them carefully.

When you're working with fabric and paint, take your time mixing colors that should match or coordinate with another element of the decor. Practice on scraps of the fabric to get a feel for how the paint works on it.

1. Once you've washed and pressed your fabric, lay it flat on a clean surface. (If the fabric is very sheer, first cover your work area with several thicknesses of unprinted newsprint or a thin flannel sheet. This will serve as a blotter for any paint that seeps through.)
2. Secure the fabric to the work surface with masking tape or dressmaker's pins. Fan-fold or roll up any of the fabric that extends beyond the immediate work surface so that it is positioned in front of the area you'll be stenciling. Always work by moving stenciled fabric *away* from you, allowing it to drape unfolded over the opposite end of your work surface as it dries.
3. Mark guidelines for the print(s) with a removable fabric pen or tailor's chalk.
4. Affix the stencil to the fabric with masking tape or repositionable spray adhesive.
5. Follow the basic stenciling procedure outlined in "Basic Techniques" (see pages 26–31). Using a very dry brush, begin stenciling on an uncut portion of the stencil, gradually pulling paint into the window. Focus of vision (see page 26) is absolutely essential in fabric stenciling because a heavy, clogged print is very unappealing and smudged edges are next to impossible to correct. On the other hand, shading and texturing effects are very easy to achieve on fabric. The paints dry quickly so that subsequent overlays can be printed almost immediately.
6. Let the print dry thoroughly (at least three to five days) before setting it with heat. You can heat-set large pieces of fabric by tumble-drying them on the high-heat setting of your clothes dryer.

### WORKING WITH SPRAY PAINTS AND AIRBRUSH

Airbrush and spray paints are both excellent means for producing delicate, shaded prints on fabric. Their primary advantage is that only air and paint touch the surface. If you're working with an airbrush, make sure that the paint is airbrush-compatible and is either formulated specifically for use on fabric or can be mixed with a textile medium. As with other types of fabric paints, most must be heat-set for permanence.

When working with airbrush and spray paints, it is particularly important that the surface of the fabric be pressed and wrinkle free. To produce a uniform print with spray paints, support the fabric in a vertical position by pinning it to a piece of heavy cardboard and leaning it against a wall. It is recommended that the areas of fabric not being stenciled as well as any surrounding areas be carefully masked or protected, as fabric is especially liable to "grab" overspray.

To avoid breathing harmful fumes and to prevent the accumulation of paint in the lungs, it is absolutely essential that goggles and a respirator or safety mask be worn at all times. In addition, you should always work in a well-ventilated area. For more information on stenciling with airbrush, see page 106.

## CORRECTING MISTAKES

The best advice for correcting mistakes on fabric is simply to let them alone. Attempts to remove mistakes, reprint, or conceal smudged edges by enlarging motifs usually only make such problems worse.

Stenciling mistakes on fabric are most commonly caused by smudges picked up from dirty hands or the backs of stencils. Keep your work area very clean, and designate a place for your working stencils and another for your palette and brushes. Above all, work slowly and carefully.

*Several yards of dotted Swiss were first stenciled with a precut wall border and perched bird accents, then constructed to fit the bassinet. Stencil designed by Adele Bishop; stenciled by Jane Gauss.*

(Above) This valance, whose stencil motifs were inspired by the fabric designs of the arts and crafts movement, was stenciled with airbrush, which works well even on fabrics with a slight texture or nap. Designed and stenciled by Sheri Hoeger. (Right) In this unusual combination of wall appliqué and stenciling, primary colors were used to create a lively nursery motif. After the fabric for the applique was cut out and applied to the wall with Mod-Podge®, squiggles were stenciled ascending toward the ceiling, where a freize of jacks-in-the-box at a smaller scale encircles the room. Designed and stenciled by Lu Ann Anderson.

*A small ribbon motif was enlarged and adapted as a stencil for napkins, potholders, and an apron, as well as notecards and flower pots. (For more information on decorative accessories, see page 93.) Designed and stenciled by Caroline Ann Zarrilli.*

# STENCILED QUILTS

The first sixty years of the 19th century witnessed the development of two trends in American folk art. The first was wall stenciling, which initially adorned only the homes of the wealthy, followed by the stenciled quilt. Both movements were centered in the New England states. Men usually stenciled walls and women stenciled quilts, and although they used similar techniques, their distinct means of expression moved their art in different directions.

The quilters of the 1820s knew they had stumbled on a unique approach to quiltmaking that also featured the best aspects of the craft of decorative painting. Many of the early stenciled quilts, which were intended for decoration rather than warmth, were both unlined and unquilted. Later, when these quilts were layered with batting and handquilted, quilters discovered that the quilting stitches gave the stenciled designs a three-dimensional look that duplicated the effects of fine appliqué, whose techniques can be both tedious and time-consuming. The motifs of

these quilts were quite simple, sometimes almost naive in style. Popular subjects like flowers, fruits, and birds were often inspired by costly imported chintz fabrics from England or India. While wall stencilers preferred to cut their stencils from stiff leather or thin metal, most quilters used heavy oiled papers.

Splendid examples of stenciled spreads and quilts can be seen in museums throughout the United States, including the Winterthur Museum in Winterthur, Delaware; the Shelburne Museum in Shelburne, Vermont; the Rockefeller Folk Art Center in Williamsburg, Virginia; the Henry Ford Museum in Dearborn, Michigan; and the Museum of American Folk Art in New York City.

If you don't have any sewing experience and would like to create your own stenciled quilt, your local bookstore and library are excellent resources for books on quiltmaking. When stenciling your quilt top, refer to the instructions on pages 78–79 for stenciling fabrics.

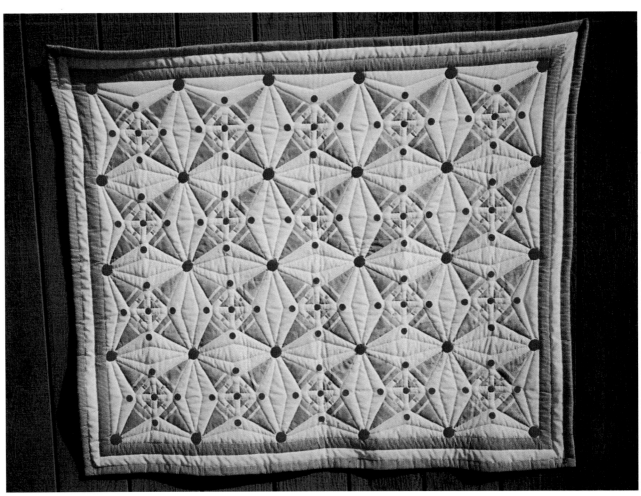

*Stylized Christmas trees in groups of four form white four-pointed stars on this whole-cloth quilt. The intense colors of the motifs were achieved with a pouncing technique. After drying and heat-setting, the stencils were all outline-quilted, then a narrow diamond shape was added to the white space between the tree "squares" to increase the dimensional effect and improve the distribution of stitching over the face of the quilt. "O Tannenbaum" quilt designed and stenciled by Marie Sturmer.*

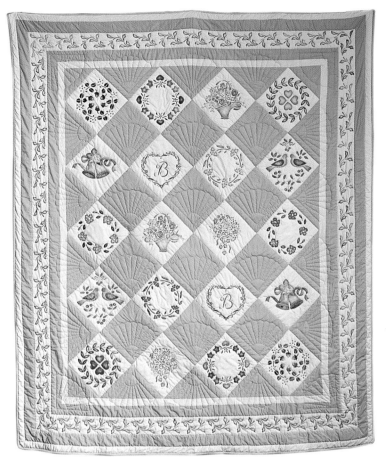

In this family heirloom quilt, each stenciled block has a specific sentimental value. A fan stencil was used as the template for the quilting stitches in the pink squares. Quilt designed and stenciled by P. J. Tetreault.

A quilted wall hanging is an effective accessory in a country-theme decor. Pure muslin was stenciled with brushes and solid paints, then cut into squares and pieced into the quilt. Quilting stitches were confined to the dark green print fabric. Designed and stenciled by Julia Hierl Burmesch for American Traditional.

# CANVAS FLOORCLOTHS

Floorcloths, which are painted canvas floor coverings, first became popular in 18th-century Europe, where they were used as a decorative alternative to rugs. In the United States during the late 1700s and early 1800s, canvas floorcloth was often the only covering over clay or dirt floors in settler's homes.

Used for centuries as a support for oil paintings, canvas is an ideal surface for stenciling. Canvas is graded by weight—the higher the number, the lighter the weight—with #8 and #10 weights most suitable for floorcloth. Pre-gessoed (already primed) canvas is available in #10 weight, but if you want to start with raw canvas use #10 instead of #8.

In addition to serving as a support for floorcloth or placemats, canvas can be stenciled and framed or mounted on walls or ceilings.

## PREPARING RAW CANVAS

Raw canvas must be coated with gesso before stenciling to even out its surface and protect it from wear.

1. Cut off the selvages prior to priming to avoid wrinkling or shrinking as the canvas dries.
2. Apply two coats of gesso with a low-nap roller, allowing adequate drying time between coats.
3. After the second coat has dried, lightly sand the canvas with extra-fine sandpaper or a crumpled brown paper bag, then wipe it with a tack cloth to remove any residue. Your canvas is now ready for basecoating.

## BASECOATING PRIMED CANVAS

Canvas can be basecoated with an oil- or water-based flat or eggshell-finish interior paint.

1. Apply two coats of paint, allowing the first coat to dry thoroughly. Do *not* paint the back of the canvas.
2. Allow the second coat to dry for at least 24 hours before stenciling.

## STENCILING CANVAS

1. Measure and mark the hem with a light-colored chalk pencil. On floorcloth, allow at least a 1-inch hem. On placemats, a $1/2$- to $3/4$-inch hem is adequate. Mark the hem on the front of the piece.
2. Determine the placement of the design using paper proofs. If you're using a gridded layout, begin measuring at the center of the canvas and work toward its outer edges.
3. Stencil your motifs.
4. To create a border around the edges of the canvas or as a part of the stenciled design, affix parallel strips of low-tack masking tape or painter's tape, making sure their edges are secure. Apply paint in the space between the strips with a small brush or a paper towel lightly dipped in paint and blotted.

## HEMMING CANVAS

After the stenciling has dried completely, crease the hem marked with the chalk pencil, fold it under, then mitre the corners and glue the hem as follows:

- *Folding corners:* Crease each side of the cloth, folding the hem all the way out to the edges of the floorcloth. Fold the corners up and and realign the creases with adjacent sides. Press the resulting triangular piece under, then cut it off. The side hems will fold perfectly without creating bulk at the corners, which can cause the canvas to curl up at the edges.
- *Gluing:* Apply an even coat of quick-drying fabric adhesive or glue to the wrong side of the canvas within the creased area. Using a rolling pin, crease and roll one side at a time, assuring that all air pockets are removed. To prevent buckling, clamp the canvas to a tabletop or lay it flat on the floor and weight the edges evenly. Allow the hemmed edges to dry overnight before applying finish coats.

## FINISHING THE FLOORCLOTH

Because of the wear and tear most floorcloths receive, they should be finished with several coats of satin-finish, water-based urethane. (Oil-based finishes yellow with time.)

1. Mist the stenciled surface with acrylic spray sealer to ensure that the stencil paint will not bleed when the varnish is applied. Let dry.
2. Remove all dust from the canvas with a tack cloth.
3. Apply the finish with a sponge brush, an oil-based bristle brush, or a low-nap roller. Work in one direction, slightly overlapping each stroke. (Avoid the inclination to use a back-and-forth stroke.) If you're using a brush, do not wipe excess finish off the brush on the rim of the can. This will cause bubbles to appear in the finish. Let the first coat dry completely before applying the second. (Under humid conditions, allow an additional six to eight hours of drying time between coats.)
4. After the second coat is completely dry, lightly sand the surface with a crumpled piece of brown paper bag, then tack it.
5. Repeat the procedure until you have applied three to five coats of finish. After the final coat has dried, lightly rub the surface with #0000 steel wool, then tack it.

## BACKING THE FLOORCLOTH

Floorcloths can be very dangerous when placed over smooth surfaces such as waxed, wood, or stone floors. To minimize the possibility of sliding, back the floorcloth with a coat of liquid rug latex or secure strips of double-faced carpet tape around its perimeter. You can also use a thin jute pad (the kind used under oriental rugs) cut 1 inch smaller than the floorcloth's finished dimensions. For placemats, no special backing is required.

## STORING A FLOORCLOTH

If you have the storage space to accommodate it, it's best to store painted canvas flat. If necessary, roll the floorcloth with the design to the inside. Rolling it into a tight cylinder or subjecting it to extreme temperatures under storage will increase the risk of cracking. Do not attempt to unroll the floorcloth unless the canvas is at room temperature.

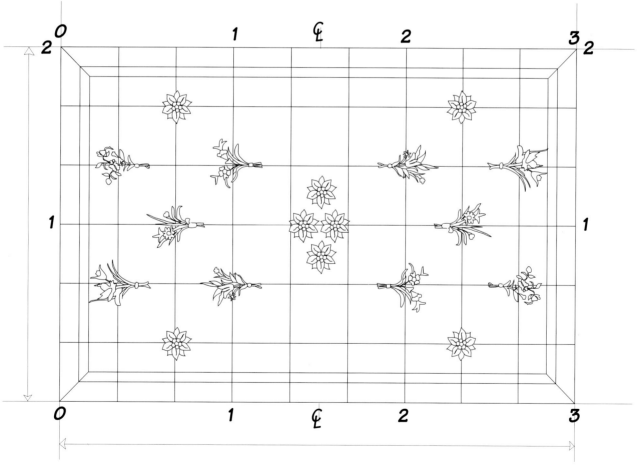

*(Top) This 2 × 3 foot trompe l'oeil tile floorcloth is mounted on Komatex board, which is another way to prolong its life and eliminate edge curling and rippling problems. (Bottom) The gridded layout shows how the design motifs were distributed in a symmetrical pattern over the surface of the floorcloth, using the intersecting lines of "grout" as guidelines. Designed and painted by Diane Patricia Rich.*

Photographs of indigenous fish and a book about antique fishing tackle were the sources for the stencil motifs of this angler's floorcloth. On a 3 × 5 foot piece of #10 canvas primed with three coats of off-white latex paint, the areas within the curved border were painted with washes of blue, green, and beige acrylic paint to simulate water. The motifs were stenciled with acrylic paints, then the floorcloth was finished with three coats of water-based urethane. Designed and stenciled by Lee Anne Miller.

A piece of 31 × 50 inch #10 weight acrylic-primed canvas basecoated with creamy off-white latex paint provides a luminous ground for the freeform botanical motifs strewn over this springtime floorcloth. The completed cloth was finished with five coats of water-based urethane. Fringe and border stencils designed by Carol Martell; flower stencils designed by Dee Keller; stenciled by Barbara N. Johnson.

Pudgy pigs and meandering flowers and vines are whimsically juxtaposed in a matching floorcloth and director's chairs. The 48 × 70 inch #10 canvas was primed with acrylic, then sponged with a dusty pink. After stenciling, the floorcloth was finished with five coats of water-based urethane, sanding lightly between coats. The chair cloth, which is similar in texture and weight to the floorcloth, was finished in the same way. Jasmine, iris vines, sweet pea, and butterfly stencils designed by Dee Keller; pig stencils designed by Nancy Tribolet; floorcloth and chairs designed and stenciled by Barbara N. Johnson.

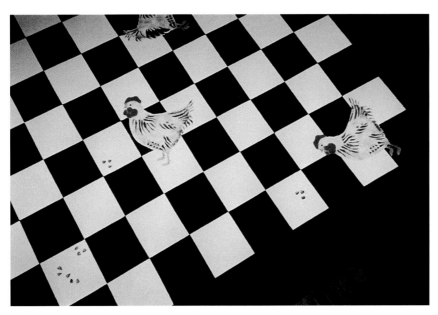

A flock of chickens scratching for feed on a checkerboard floor graces this unusual floorcloth. Following a basecoat of gesso and two coats of flat white acrylic paint, the cloth (awning-weight canvas) was hemmed and glued. The border was measured and marked with masking tape, then three coats of dark green latex paint were applied. After the border had dried thoroughly, the squares were measured and masked. Because the cloth is textured, it was necessary to use the edge of a credit card to ensure a feather-proof line. The chicken and feed stencils were sponged with a cosmetic sponge and allowed to dry for three days before finishing with four coats of water-based urethane slightly thinned with water. Designed and stenciled by Patricia Flournoy.

# CERAMIC TILE

Ceramic tile has recently become extremely popular as a means for decorative expression in the home. To create a permanent high-traffic surface, both glazed and unglazed tiles must be painted with ceramic paints, then carefully fired in a kiln and installed by a professional tile installer. Stenciling classes for ceramic tile are always well attended at the yearly SALI conventions, and the step-by-step photographs shown opposite are from a class given by Carol Phippen featuring designs by Susan Saye and paints by Harrison-Bell. (The stencil patterns for these tiles appear on page 130.)

If you're unfamiliar with the process of firing and you don't have access to a kiln, or if you intend to work on only one or two tile projects at the most and don't want to invest in ceramic paints or a kiln of your own, you might want to consider the possibility of renting studio time and/or kiln space at a local ceramics studio. Many studios offer such services, and your project is sure to benefit from the owner's or manager's knowledge about firing.

Newly developed paints and primers have also made it possible to stencil ceramic tile that is already in place. This type of application is only appropriate for an area that will not receive heavy wear, such as a counter backsplash or a decorative tile wall, but is not recommended for tubs, sinks, showers, or floor tiles. An example of this type of tile stenciling appears on page 92.

## STENCILING TILE

In some significant respects, the process of stenciling ceramic tiles differs from the standard stenciling procedure. First and foremost, *only* ceramic studio paints can be used on glazed tiles that will be subsequently fired and installed. If you use Harrison-Bell paints, you'll need to mix them with high-gloss sealer to maintain paint consistency and to ensure that they dry completely. Although the sealer is white, it dries clear and will not affect paint color. The sealer's label advises "do not fire," but firing doesn't seem to have an adverse effect on paint mixed with sealer. After mixing sealer into the paint, you have about 15 minutes to use the paint before it dries.

In contrast to most other surfaces, the stencil applicator should carry a fairly heavy load of paint. Do *not* blot excess paint from the applicator on a paper towel before working in into the window. Because the paint can't be absorbed by the tile's hard glazed surface, it's relatively easy to correct mistakes or make changes before the tiles are fired: Simply wash or wipe off the paint and begin again. (Note that prints can't be corrected or changed after firing.)

1. Spray the back of the stencil very lightly with repositionable spray adhesive, then place it face up on a clean sheet of paper. This is done to prevent dust from collecting on the sprayed side that could be transferred to the painting surface.
2. Using a palette knife, mix the first color on a piece of glass. (Glass is preferred because ceramic paints will stain a plastic palette.) Be sure to mix enough paint for the entire job. A few words of caution about red: In contrast to all other colors, red will not fire to the same color that is mixed. Also, the glass will make reds seem both bluer and darker than they actually are.
3. Transfer a small amount of paint for the first overlay onto a second sheet of glass. Use a palette knife to mix a few drops of high-gloss sealer into the paint. (The amount of sealer you add depends on the amount of paint you have to mix.) The paint should be the consistency of heavy cream.
4. Load the applicator and stencil the print. After the paint dries (in 4 to 5 minutes), you can apply a second coat to deepen the color or shade with another color. If you need more paint to finish the first stencil overlay, transfer another small amount of paint from the first glass palette to the second and add the sealer. Any remaining paint that has not been mixed with sealer can be stored in a container and revived by adding a few drops of water.
5. When the paint is dry to the touch, remove the first overlay and position the second. Repeat the procedure until the print is complete.
6. If necessary, correct any run-unders with your thumb or a moist paper towel. If the run-under is too large to fix, you probably added too much sealer to the paint.
7. Use an artist's brush to fill in any gaps resulting from a faulty stencil or to add details like highlights or shading.
8. Clean both stencils and applicators immediately using soap and water. Allow applicators to dry thoroughly before reusing.

## FIRING STENCILED TILES

Fire the stenciled tiles with a #16 cone. Kiln cones, which are used to measure the heat inside a kiln, are made of various blends of ceramic materials that melt and deform at specific temperatures.

1. Place the stenciled tiles in the kiln by laying them down flat on a shelf or stacking them upright on a rack without touching each other or the sides of the kiln. (As reds and pinks fire to different shades at different temperatures, place all of the tiles containing red or pink on the same shelf.) Place one shelf on top of the other, with no less than an inch of space between shelves. Do not plug holes at any time during firing.
2. With the lid open 1 inch, set the kiln to low for 1 hour, then increase the heat to medium for a second hour.
3. Close the lid and turn heat to high until kiln reaches desired heat and the cone melts or the kiln shuts off.
4. With the lid closed, let cool for three times as long as the firing time.
5. After the first firing, you can paint over any or all of the colors if you're dissatisfied with the results. (Deep reds almost always require a second coat of paint and a second firing.) With the print already in place, it's generally unnecessary to affix the stencil to the tile the second time around. Using an artist's brush and water as a mixing medium, simply paint the second coat freehand.

1. Mix ceramic paints to the desired shades, transfer a small amount of each to another surface, then add high-gloss sealer.

2. Stencil tiles with a relatively heavy load of paint.

3. Remove the stencil, let the paint dry, then stencil the next overlay or color.

4. Add details with an artist's brush.

5. The stenciled tiles before firing. Stencils designed by Susan Saye; tiles stenciled by Carol Phippen. (See page 130 for stencil patterns.)

What better place for a permanent, scrubbable rug than a laundry room? No more crumpled rugs in front of the washer and dryer! Installed by a professional tiler with light gray grout, the rug's fringes were painted on lighter tiles to emphasize its length. Designed by Jane Gauss; stenciled and fired by Susan Saye. (See pages 131–135 for ivy and fringe patterns.)

The tile design in this kitchen, which was in the process of being updated with cherrywood cabinets and white 4 × 4 inch tiles above the countertops, grew out of a simple blue-gray floral pattern on a candy dish. Several stencil patterns were combined to create an overflowing basket of flowers in an alcove above the cooktop. The colors of the bouquet were chosen to complement the warm hues of the cabinetry and to introduce the desired blue-gray. Three single-color flower designs that were also based on the candy dish motif were scattered throughout the field of white tiles above the countertops. Tiles were fired once, overpainted and highlighted as needed, then refired. Tiles designed and stenciled by Patricia Fielder.

These 6 × 6 inch tiles contain both stenciled and freehand images. The motifs were first plotted on tracing paper cut to the size of the tile, then traced with a sharp pencil and graphite paper onto a blank tile, with the resulting lines used as painting guidelines. The solid forms of the images were fired first, then color corrections, outlining, highlighting, and other details were added for a second firing. This technique allows for more freedom in design and a more relaxed attitude toward both stenciling and painting. Tiles designed and stenciled by Patricia Fielder.

91

The ivy motifs on these tiles were adapted from wallpaper and designed for a scattered, all-over layout so that each would appear to be one of a kind. Each ivy pattern required three overlays, with tendrils and some of the smaller leaves painted freehand. The first two overlays were stenciled and fired, then the final overlay and details and highlight were added prior to the second firing. Tiles designed and stenciled by Patricia Fielder.

Although firing stenciled tiles prior to professional installation helps safeguard their durability, already installed tiles can also be primed, stenciled, and sealed to produce a handpainted look. These tiles can only be wiped clean, so while they are not recommended for tiled walls in showers or on floors or countertops they do work well on backsplashes in kitchens or utility areas.

Keep in mind that surface preparation—cleaning, stripping, and priming—will determine your success. Before priming the tiles, make sure they are dry and free from any grease, oil, or loose paint or dirt. If necessary, clean them with strong detergent, rinse thoroughly, then wipe them down with XIM Gone (do not use solvents that contain mineral spirits). Apply a primer/bonder made specifically for tile with a brush or roller, then basecoat the area with latex paint. (The background in this example was sponged on to create an underwater look.) After stenciling, paint the motifs with at least three coats of water-based polyurethane. Installed glazed tile primed, painted, and stenciled by Maureen Soens.

# ACCESSORIES

Accessories complete the look of a room by adding finishing touches of color, texture and design. You can stencil an object (or several) to create a theme or to duplicate motifs you've stenciled elsewhere. You can also adapt motifs from an accessory to set the tone of an entire decor. As you look through the photographs in this book, take note of how accessories can be used to create inviting interiors.

It can be extremely satisfying to transform a plain, dull, or forgotten object into one that creates color and interest in a decor. Stenciled accessories make ideal gifts, and can even be sold at craft shows or on consignment through interior decorators. The examples shown below and on pages 94–98 are just a brief survey of the variety of looks that can be achieved.

*Accessories can serve as both venues and sources for stenciling. The wall stencils shown above, which decorate a country French kitchen, were adapted from an extensive collection of antique Quimper pottery, which was first produced in the late 1600s. The pottery designs were traced and enlarged to appropriate dimensions. Motifs were shaded in several colors to achieve a handpainted look. To protect them during cleaning, the finished motifs were misted with matte sealer. Design adapted and stenciled by Anita Alsup.*

*The stencil motifs on the tiles and placemat are Pfaltzgraff designs licensed by American Traditional. Each of the stencil patterns offered coordinates with a popular stoneware pattern. Designed and stenciled by Judith Barker of American Traditional.*

*Create a one-of-a-kind decorator accent by block-printing a lampshade with rose and vine motifs. First, spray the shade with one or two even coats of cream-colored acrylic spray paint. Load the block with glaze, and starting at the lampshade's back seam, support the area to be blocked with one hand while pressing down on the blocking pad with the other. Before reloading the block, randomly press the pad on the shade two or three more times to create bunches of leaves. Repeat the process to print leaves around the circumference of the shade. To add rosebuds, brush the pad with two pink glazes and a bit of green at its base. For each rosebud, press the pad near or among the leaves. Wash off the rosebud pad with a wet soapy cloth, then use it to add smaller leaves around the top of the shade. Use an artist's brush loaded with green glaze to add vines connecting leaves and flowers. Let dry for at least 16 hours, then spray the shade with a clear lacquer. Designed and block-printed by Vi and Stu Cutbill.*

(Above and left) Caroline Ann Zarrilli uses stencils to coordinate accessories for bath, kitchen, and sunroom.

# PAPER AND CANVAS PRINTS

Since you've begun all your projects by proofing stencils on paper, it probably won't require a great leap of the imagination to envision your designs as framed prints. Instead of using paper scraps or blank newsprint, you'll want to purchase paper in an appropriate weight (at least 140 lbs.) or perhaps an unusual color.

If you've worked with canvas to make a floorcloth or placemats, or even if you're just an oil painting aficionado, you already know that canvas is an excellent support for paint. If the thought of working on canvas intimidates you, practice on paper until you've perfected your stenciled work of art.

*Although theorem stencils were traditionally stenciled on white or off-white velvet, they also look beautiful on watercolor paper. This four-overlay botanical rose was stenciled on 140-lb. hot-pressed (smooth surface) watercolor paper. To enhance the handpainted look of the design, each overlay was shaded from light to dark. The finished work was then matted, framed, and "hung" from a stenciled tasseled cord. Designed and stenciled by Julia Hierl Burmesch. (For more information on theorem stencils, see page 108.)*

*This heart-shaped wreath, which measures 36 × 39 inches, was stenciled with airbrush on artist's canvas. The cut-out pieces of some of the leaves were applied randomly over the surface of the canvas, which was then sprayed lightly with yellow, pink, and blue for a misty background effect. When the cut-outs were removed, their negative images were left as guides for painting. The design was then stenciled, stretched, and framed. Designed and stenciled by Sheri Hoeger.*

# EMBOSSED AND PIERCED PAPER

As demonstrated by Judith Barker of American Traditional, stencils can be used to create intricate embossed and pierced designs quickly and easily. Although brass stencils are featured in the sequence of step-by-step photographs below, any type of stencil can be used for these purposes. You can also use just about any weight of paper for these projects, but note that the thicker the paper, the deeper the embossed relief.

Combine several stencil patterns to create your own designs. You can decorate note cards, gift tags, lamp shades, ornaments, and bookmarks, to name just a few possibilities.

1. Place the stencil on the paper and secure it with two small pieces of masking tape. To reduce excess tack, stick the tape to your clothes a few times (avoid woolly sweaters).

2. Flip the paper over and place it over a light source such as a light table, a window illuminated by daylight, or a TV screen.

3. Trace the outline of the stencil with an embossing tool or stylus. (A knitting needle or crochet hook will also work.) To pierce the paper, trace either all or part of a selected motif with an X-Acto knife.

4. Once you've finished tracing, the embossing or piercing is complete. At this point you can either carefully remove the stencil from the paper, or if you'd like to add stenciling, turn the paper over and stencil in the motifs. Acrylics, poster paints, watercolors, oil pastels, stamp pad ink, and stencil creams can all be used to add color. In any event, use very little paint, taking care to thoroughly wipe the brush on a piece of scrap paper before applying it to the stencil window.

3

1

2

1. Attach the stencil to the paper with low-tack tape.
2. Flip the paper over, then trace the motifs with a stylus over a light source.
3. Before removing the stencil, turn the paper over to add stenciling if desired.

*A set of recipe cards were embossed and stenciled to match a recipe box and table linens. Designed, embossed, and stenciled by Judith Barker of American Traditional.*

*An embossed, pierced, and stenciled lampshade offers home decorators an opportunity to create a unique custom accessory. You can stencil a ready-made paper shade or make one yourself. Stencils from American Traditional; embossed, pierced, and stenciled by Judith Barker.*

# STENCILING OUTDOORS

Don't confine your stenciling talents to your home's interior! While the stenciling techniques are the same, as with most other surfaces the key to an exterior print's resistance to wear (in this case, the elements) is surface preparation, choice of paints for stenciling, and finishing products. High-quality exterior latex paints are all formulated for extended durability and to resist peeling and fading, in many cases eliminating the need for a finish coat.

*This delicate floral garland gracing a front entrance was stenciled with acrylic stencil paints over a basecoat of latex exterior paint. The completed prints were then finished with a light rose glaze that not only protects the surface but visually connects the prints, the burgundy door, and the floral wreath that adorns it. Designed and stenciled by Elizabeth Hurbis.*

*Create a botanical point of interest wherever foliage is lacking by adding a meandering stenciled vine. The rambling vine on these painted shingles was stenciled with exterior latex paint, so no protective finish was required. Designed and stenciled by Linda Radziminski.*

Antique wooden doors open onto a traditional Spanish-style courtyard in this southern California home. Framing this beautiful entrance are stenciled freeform bougainvillea branches that appear at first glance to be growing over the walls and down the sides of the doorway. The stucco walls, which were painted with flat exterior paint, were cleaned thoroughly before the designs were applied with artist's acrylics. The petals were stenciled with the reds and purples of the real bougainvillea growing on either side of the entrance. Because of harsh sun exposure and concern about yellowing and cracking, no finish coat was applied. Designed and stenciled by Melanie Royals.

How do you leave the charm and character of a 100-year-old house and move into a new one that lacks personality? (In defense of new homes, it could be argued that the 100-year-old house was also considered to be short on personality when it was first built.) This stenciler adapted a traditional pattern into a border to project a sense of fun and style onto a relatively drab stucco exterior. Exterior latex paint was applied with a pouncing stroke on the heavily textured surface. No finish was required. Designed and stenciled by Jo Miller.

*This white-and-hunter-green checkerboard "rug" was stenciled with deck stain on pretreated wood. The squares were measured, outlined with a chalk line, then taped. The white stain was painted first, then the tape was removed and the green stain was added to match the umbrella. Designed and stenciled by Anne Rullman and Lynn Terrel.*

*A freeform stencil garden combined with real potted plants enlivens the stucco facade of a small guest cottage while minimizing weeding and watering. Following a fresh coat of exterior house paint, the stencils were airbrushed with acrylics, then any fogging resulting from the rough surface was touched up by hand. The prints were randomly stacked to create a dimensional look. After 24 hours, the stenciling was sealed with matte spray varnish containing a UV protectant that won't discolor or yellow. Stencils designed by Dee Keller; stenciled by Stephanie A. Crabb.*

The plain stucco walls of a garage have been utterly transformed by several eye-catching trompe l'oeil techniques that combine stenciling and freehand painting. The surface of the stucco was prepared with a coat of white exterior paint, then stenciled with exterior latex paints. The illusion of reality is so strong that it's difficult to determine what is real and what is painted. Note how shadowing is used to give stenciled prints the visual depth that trompe l'oeil requires. (Top) This side of the garage features a girl and boy playing hide and seek, irises, a watering can, climbing vines, and a faux door, exposed bricks, and shutters. (Center) On this wall, stenciled birdhouses are situated among real hanging baskets of flowers. (Bottom) In this detail, frogs splash in a bucket of water while trying to catch monarch butterflies. (For more information on trompe l'oeil, see page 114.) Designed and stenciled by Laurie Spagnolia.

# EXTERIOR ACCESSORIES

If the prospect of stenciling the side of a building overwhelms your sense of commitment, keep in mind that there are other, less taxing ways to display your stenciling talents out-of-doors. As shown in the examples below, you can reduce the scale of your project without limiting your creativity.

In many cases, the proposed surface will be a natural one such as stone or metal, whose intrinsic beauty can only be enhanced by stenciling. With these materials, priming, bonding, and sealing procedures are of the utmost importance. To begin with the wrong foundation or end with the wrong finish only invites trouble, particularly when a project must endure a whole spectrum of climatic conditions.

Check with your local paint store and ask them to recommend products for these surfaces. Products by XIM, which specializes in the manufacture of priming, bonding, and finishing products for metal and stone, are distributed through many retail outlets. (See page 140 for contact information.)

*A utilitarian object can also serve to express your style and talent. This prefinished white mailbox was primed with XIM Clear 400 Flash bond, then stenciled with acrylic paints. (The bows and ribbons required a small amount of freehand work.) The project was finished with two coats of nonyellowing clear finish to protect it from the elements. Designed and stenciled by P. J. Tetreault.*

*Antique roofing slates supplied by local roofers can be stenciled as welcome plaques. After scrubbing the slate with a stiff brush, the surface was checked for flaking. (The slate should be free from cracks and blemishes.) When completely dry, stenciling was done with acrylic paints. (Since the lobster didn't show up well on the slate's dark surface, a white oval ground was painted first.) The stenciling was allowed to dry for at least 24 hours, then the slate was painted both front and back with one coat of exterior water-based varnish. A masonry bit was used to drill holes for a leather rawhide strip for hanging. Designed and stenciled by Lee Anne Miller.*

*A limestone backsplash above a cooktop provides an excellent venue for an airbrushed basket of fruit. The design was adapted from the fabric that decorates the kitchen. (For more information on stenciling with airbrush, and for more details on this project, see pages 106–107.) Designed and stenciled by Sheri Hoeger.*

# ADVANCED TECHNIQUES

If you've mastered basic application and cutting techniques, experimented with various styles and surfaces, and successfully completed a few stenciling projects, you're probably thinking about inventing new challenges for yourself. By increasing the intricacy of images and expanding the pictorial scope of your projects, you will ensure your creative growth.

This chapter examines the ways in which stenciling is used to create complex, compelling images that both imitate and capitalize on the nuances that can be achieved with handpainting. Airbrushing is an alternate method for applying paint that produces extraordinarily delicate shadings and color blends. Theorem stenciling uses several intricately cut overlays to eliminate the gaps that appear between the motifs of conventional stencils. With the potential to turn an entire room into an artist's canvas, trompe l'oeil attempts to simulate reality (or create a convincing fantasy) by combining stenciling and handpainting techniques with the use of perspective and the representation of light and shadow. This pictorial approach is historically linked to the ancient art of mural painting, in which mostly amateur artists sought to transport their audiences beyond the boundaries of a room or dwelling.

# STENCILING WITH AIRBRUSH

Originally developed in the late 19th century and customarily used by commercial artists to produce elaborate illustrations of soft, fluid color, airbrush is a relatively recent addition to the stenciler's arsenal of techniques. As with other methods of stenciling, airbrush applies paint in small amounts a layer at a time, blending colors and building intensity and depth as each layer is added. But with the fine spray of airbrush, stencilers can also create subtle effects of color once possible only with freehand painting.

Note that the airbrush stenciling techniques illustrated by the masterful work of airbrush artist Sheri Hoeger can also be used with aerosol spray paints. Examples of Sheri's work can also be seen on pages 63, 68, 80, and 96.

## EQUIPMENT

An airbrush dispenses a fine spray of paint through a nozzle or needle by means of compressed air. The force of the spray is regulated by the amount of pressure exerted on the trigger as well as the distance between the nozzle and the stenciled surface. The width and fineness of the spray can also be varied by changing spray heads or needles and by varying the amount of air pressure from the compressor.

While the spray pattern of a single-action airbrush can't be altered during painting, the trigger of a dual-action airbrush can be manipulated to vary the flow of both air (by pressing it down) and paint (by pulling it back). In either case, you'll need an airbrush equipped with a cap for the color cup or jar. Use tape to secure the cap, taking care not to cover the tiny air hole that equalizes the pressure in the color cup.

There are many different types of compressors on the market. Although for some small projects you can use compressed air in cans or even a spare tire as a short-term air source, a compressor made specifically for airbrush would be the most efficient source. For larger jobs and heavier use, you'll need a compressor with an air holding tank that is still light enough to be portable. These vary widely in price and the amount of noise they produce, so contact hardware and art supply stores in your area for more information.

To keep paint and fumes from damaging your lungs, a respirator or a safety mask must be worn while using an airbrush. The Respro Mask is more comfortable than a respirator and more effective than a dust mask.

## AIRBRUSH PAINTS

The type of paint you use must be compatible not only with the surface you're stenciling—for example, fabrics should be stenciled with fabric paints or with paints to which a textile medium has been added—but should also contain finely ground pigment to accommodate its flow through the airbrush. In addition to airbrush paints, which are pre-thinned to proper airbrush viscosity, acrylic gouache thinned to a milky consistency is suitable for walls. You might want to try adding a flow medium to break the tension in the paint, which will also help prevent clogging on the tip.

Due to slow drying times and harmful airborne toxins, oil-based paints are not recommended for use with an airbrush. If you choose to spray oil-based paint or lacquer, make sure that your work area is well ventilated and that you wear a respirator approved for those products.

## USING AN AIRBRUSH

Before you start your first project, it's important to practice using the airbrush so you can get a "feel" for what you can achieve with it. When learning any new skill it takes time to develop confidence and ability, so be patient with yourself. Follow the manufacturer's instructions, and try different ways of shading and controlling the paint spray. The edges of the stencil must be masked to prevent overspray, especially at ceiling lines, corners, or other areas where paint might collect. Use repositionable stencil adhesive to prevent overspray from causing "ghosted" or blurred prints. If the surface is textured, you may need to press down on the edge of the window before spraying to make a sharp-edged print.

Begin by spraying on the uncut portion of the stencil, then move smoothly into the window. Rather than swiveling your wrist, move your hand and arm together. For light and subtle shading, spray along the edge of the window, allowing just the overspray to paint the surface.

As always, make paper proofs to test different shading variations and to make sure that the colors you've chosen work well together. Note that colors tend to look slightly darker after they've dried. They can be lightened before spraying by adding white or colorless extender, and darkened or muted by adding tiny amounts of black. To achieve a pleasing balance of color within a print, use colors of similar value or intensity.

If you're stenciling a wall border with only one airbrush, you'll need to work all the way around a room with each color. Sometimes this means realigning an overlay that's already been stenciled. In most cases, you can move the stencil along the wall immediately because so little paint is used and the drying time is so short. In addition to saving time when stenciling a wall, using two airbrushes will enable you to stencil two colors at a time. Compressor hardware for two airbrushes is readily available at hardware stores. A quick-connect hose system reduces time spent attaching them and when using additional hoses for lofty projects. These systems, which are also available at hardware stores, should be installed using Teflon tape as a sealant to prevent air leakage.

## OTHER APPLICATIONS

Airbrush stenciling and faux finishes complement each other beautifully. As when airbrushing wood (see page 68), you can add color and depth without obscuring the subtle shadings of the previous coats of paint or the character of the surface. You can also experiment with airbrush as a medium for faux finishes.

A variety of other surfaces, including fabrics and ceramic tiles, can be stenciled with airbrush. For more information, see "Other Stenciling Projects," pages 70–103.

This windswept tree was designed to complement the style of the furnishings and the meandering grapevine in the bedspread. After the textured wall was painted with latex paint, the area of the wall to be stenciled was covered with clear plastic adhesive film and the design was drawn on it with permanent marker. The trunk and branches were then cut out with an X-Acto knife and stenciled with airbrush, and the roots and the contours of the tree were painted freehand. The tree was airbrushed with a series of earth colors, followed by a fine layer of gold to give it a faint shimmer. The berries, leaves, and ivy were stenciled separately, with leaves billowing across the other walls. Ivy stencil designed by Jan Dressler; designed and stenciled by Sheri Hoeger.

The thin, semi-transparent layers of airbrushed color allow the natural color and "tooth," or microscopic roughness, of the unpolished limestone backsplash to become an integral part of this elegant print. Various paints were first tested on another limestone tile to determine which would adhere the best. Prior to stenciling, the backsplash was wiped down with a mixture of white vinegar and water to remove oil and dust. After the stencil print had dried, the slab was coated with a masonry sealant. Designed and stenciled by Sheri Hoeger.

# THEOREM STENCILING

The term "theorem painting" has traditionally been used to refer to a type of stenciling done on white cotton velveteen that was popular in the United States during the 19th century. Theorem stencils, which require a series of intricately cut overlays, were designed to eliminate space between motif components, thus producing images of great complexity.

The intricacy of theorem designs made the task of cutting them by hand daunting and die-cutting extremely difficult and cost prohibitive, leading to an unfortunate decline in this unusual form of stenciling. The development of laser-cutting technology, which makes precise, highly detailed precut stencils both easily accessible and affordable, has generated new interest in theorem stenciling. As a result, "theorem stenciling" is now used to refer to the design, cutting, and stenciling of intricate, bridgeless prints, rather than to the surface on which they are stenciled.

## BASIC PROCEDURE

For your first try at theorem stenciling, it is recommended that you work with a precut design. It's not unusual for even experienced stencil cutters to feel more than a little intimidated by the demands of cutting a theorem design.

Place each stencil over the full-size color reproduction of the sample finished print. This will help you to determine to which part of the design each window corresponds. Pay particular attention to how each area is shaded, then continue to refer back to the sample print as you stencil to verify the location and intensity of the shading.

1. Position Stencil #1 so that the design is centered on the surface to be stenciled. The easiest way to do this is to stack all the stencil overlays together (with Stencil #1 on the bottom), center the entire design on the surface, carefully remove all the overlays except for Stencil #1, then secure it to the surface with stenciling tape.

2. Load the applicator with paint, then remove excess on a paper towel. As you apply paint, remember that there are two ways to achieve shading: (1) by gradually increasing the pressure on the applicator as you stencil, creating progressively darker values within a motif; and (2) by working from light to dark, applying "layers" of two or more colors, concentrating the darker values in the shaded areas, until you achieve the desired contrast and intensity. Using the color progressions listed in the instructions, apply paint with a circular stroke, working from the edges of each motif toward its center. All areas and color progressions on Stencil #1 *must* be completed before you move on to Stencil #2.

3. After completing Stencil #1, remove it from the surface and align the motifs of Stencil #2 with those that were just painted. Repeat the procedure described in step 2 until all the overlays have been stenciled.

4. If there are any gaps between stenciled areas, reapply the appropriate stencil, shift it slightly to accommodate the gap, and blend with a clean applicator. If you'd like to add more dimension to leaves, you can create a center vein by placing a curved piece of Mylar or stencil vellum along the center of each leaf and lightly brush along the curve with a contrasting shade of green. If more detail is desired, add veins to the leaves with a liner brush loaded with thinned paint.

*These unusual flowers were adapted from fabric to create a theorem stencil. Designed and stenciled by P. J. Tetreault.*

These step-by-step
sequences showing
the development
of two images—an
Old World Santa
and a June rose—
illustrate how
theorem stencils use
several overlays to
create complex,
bridgeless images.
Designed and
stenciled by Jean
Hansen.

An exotic bouquet comprised of several individual theorem images, including a bird of paradise, an orchid, and a hibiscus, are the focal point of a bedroom's decor. A liner brush was used to add only a few of the finest details. Designed and stenciled by P. J. Tetreault.

# CREATING VOLUME WITH SHADOWS

Along with highlighting and shading, shadows are used to create depth and volume in stenciled motifs. An object that casts a shadow appears to have form and mass; thus, shadows are added to stenciled motifs to enhance their realism and clarify their presence within a space. Depending on where and how it is used, a stenciled shadow should take into account the direction and quality of the existing light source so that it doesn't conflict visually with those cast by actual objects. Also, shadows on motifs that are adjacent to each other should cast shadows of similar quality and length.

As is evidenced by airbrush artist Sheri Hoeger's floorcloth (shown below), shadows can be used to dramatic effect. Although this particular floorcloth was executed with an airbrush, it isn't necessary to use one to produce shadows. (One advantage of airbrush is that the width of the spray can be precisely controlled, which permits freehand shading within the stencil window.) The key to the technique is the drop-out or cut-out portion of the stencil, which is used as a mask to create subtle shaded contours, highlights, and shadows. Shadows can also be added freehand as a detail or finishing touch.

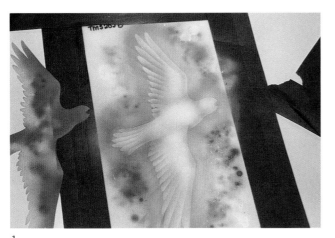

1

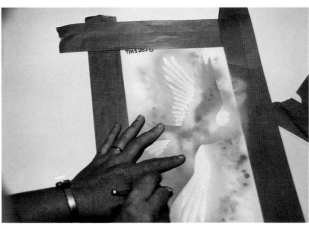

2

3

1. After the floorcloth was painted with Navajo white, the dove was stenciled with titanium white and the drop-out portion of its stencil was used to define the feathers.
2. Starting at the crook of each feather and gradually fading out toward the center of the wing, a light gray line was stenciled while pivoting the cutout slightly to make the span of the feathers appear natural. The dove's contours were then shaded across the neck and the tail. White was added to strengthen highlights and soften contours that looked a bit too defined.
3. For the shadows, the cutout was placed over the bird and light gray was airbrushed freehand following the outlines of the bird and the ribbon. Designed and stenciled by Sheri Hoeger.

The occupants of the gilded cage (above left) have been caught in the act of decorating their home with delicate wildflowers. The bird cage, which required five overlays, was stenciled with a metallic gold acrylic paint applied with a pouncing stroke for maximum coverage. The shadows on the birds (right) were stenciled very lightly in a soft gray by shifting the stencil slightly away from the light source and stenciling just along the edge of the window. The fine details were added with a liner brush. Designed and stenciled by P. J. Tetreault.

This faux brick wall and the objects it displays is located in a tiny kitchen alcove that could accommodate only the barest of furnishings. The bricks were first sponged on so that the color of the wall beneath was completely covered, then "aged" by dabbing on flecks of white with a large stencil brush. The mortar was applied by tapping on paint unevenly with a small flat brush, and a piece of cardboard cut to the size of the bricks was used to guide its alignment. After the shelf above the brick was created by sideloading a flat brush with raw umber to depict its shadow, the objects were stenciled (the flowers, vase, teapot, and plate) and handpainted (the bunny). A shadow was painted in next to each object using an artist's brush and raw umber paint thinned with extender for a more transparent look. Flowers, vase, teapot, and plate stencils designed by Dee Keller; designed, stenciled, and painted by Linda Radziminski.

*A stenciled and shadowed bleeding heart adds color to an empty space without impeding pedestrian traffic. Designed and stenciled by P. J. Tetreault.*

*A delicately shadowed fern can thrive on any wall. Designed and stenciled by P. J. Tetreault.*

# TROMPE L'OEIL

Trompe l'oeil (a French phrase meaning "deceive the eye") is a style of painting in which objects are depicted with photographically realistic detail. In addition to shading, highlighting, and shadows, trompe l'oeil artists employ the principles of perspective and a range of painting techniques to convince viewers that their illusions are real. Even when working opaquely, paint is kept to a minimum, as a visible buildup of strokes will ruin the hoax.

The photographs below and on the opposite page illustrate several trompe l'oeil treatments that incorporate stenciling. Of special interest to those facing interior design problems of scale, proportion, and space are the examples of *architectural stenciling*, a type of trompe l'oeil in which stenciling is used to produce decorative architectural elements such as moldings and columns, as well as to create the illusion of space where none actually exists.

*This elegant kimono graces the entryway to a large great room whose massive windows overlook a river. After the body of the kimono was painted in bold reds and yellows, colors were adjusted and folds created with shading to represent the effects of reflected light. Note the bonsai in the lower left, which cleverly conceals an electrical outlet. Designed and stenciled by Jo Bach Crary.*

*The accurate depiction of the direction, amount, and quality of the light as well as perspective and color balance all contribute to the success of this trompe l'oeil urn and niche on canvas. This kind of architectural stenciling can be applied to a wall or within an existing molding to create an elegant decorative touch. Designed and stenciled by Eileen Snell.*

*This trompe l'oeil rug stenciled on a hardwood floor is so realistic that visitors try to straighten out its turned-up corner. Designed and stenciled by P. J. Tetreault.*

*By manipulating value to produce highlights and shadows, multi-overlay stencils can be used to mimic fabrics such as silk damask and to create the illusion of carved moldings. This intricately patterned wall was painted with several values of flat latex wall paint, but no shading was required. Designed and stenciled by Vladimir and Olga Rozenshtein.*

# IMAGINARY VISTAS

The window is another popular architectural stenciling motif. This decorative device, which is relatively easy to stencil, is an excellent way to create light and space in a cramped room or windowless alcove. If you don't feel comfortable cutting your own stencil or painting a window freehand, there are many precut window stencils on the market, some of which include overlays for shadows. The "view" can be as simple or as complex as you'd like, and you can easily avoid problems of perspective and angle of view by stenciling or painting a simple sky dotted with distant clouds and a few vines or leaves directly "outside" the window. In more complex images, the position of the window and the shading of the images within its view are crucial to the overall effect. Try to imitate an effect of a light that is consistent with the primary light source in that particular room. If there are any actual windows in the room, note the direction and intensity of the sunlight, then try to translate the effect to your window. To add glass to your window, add a coat of high-gloss varnish to the panes to simulate its reflective qualities.

*To create a basic trompe l'oeil window, start by tracing and masking its outer dimensions, then paint in the outline with white latex paint. Place the stencil over the painted area and stencil in the sky and clouds. (This stenciler used foam rollers, a sash brush, and latex paint.) Then complete the view by adding some stenciled leaves. Use whatever paints you prefer for this stage. Remove the window stencil and add shadows to give the mullions and muttons depth. Designed and stenciled by Sandra Buckingham.*

*To create realistic stencil curtains, Sandra Buckingham uses large pieces of freezer paper cut to outline the shapes of the main fabric folds and a small stencil of the fabric pattern (such as gingham or calico). This clever technique doesn't require any freehand painting ability or experience. Designed and stenciled by Sandra Buckingham.*

*This stenciled trompe l'oeil window featuring sheer curtains blowing in an imaginary breeze was painted on canvas before being applied to a wall with paper paste. Designed and stenciled by Heather Whitehouse.*

*In this lovely "view of Provence," the arched window, cobblestones, and flowers were created with stencils, but the texture of the wall and the details of the scene required the assistance of a professional decorative painter and a fine artist. Designed and stenciled by Sharon Ranney.*

*A small alcove enclosing the tub in a master bath is the perfect spot for a view of a garden. The walls were painted white, then sponged with two shades of peach paint. After the area inside the window was masked off and painted white, the background sky and landscape were randomly dabbed on with brushes, then coated with a white latex glaze to mimic the optical effect of aerial perspective. The main window frame was masked off and painted black, then the white glaze was painted within the open panel with a small foam roller to give it a glasslike appearance. On the ledge, a watering can filled with geraniums was stenciled with some shading for volume, and leaf veins were added with a liner brush. Within the closed panel, a border stencil was turned vertically to create some interest, then the panel was glazed. The hummingbird was stenciled to appear as if it had just flown into the room. The panes within the open panel were measured and masked with tape, then painted in. Finishing touches were added by sideloading a flat brush to add shadows beneath the window and highlights to the frame and panes. Ivy and watering can stencils designed by Nancy Tribolet; hummingbird stencil by Periwinkle Designs; flowers and vine stencil designed by Adele Bishop; geraniums designed by Designer Stencils; designed and stenciled by Linda Radziminski and Mary Jane Malinoski.*

This shuttered window with faux brick accents embellishes a two-story foyer. The walls were painted with a low-luster paint, then sponged with a taupe glaze followed by a deep brown glaze to create a stucco effect. Prior to stenciling with solid paints, the area above the molding was primed with BIN 1-2-3 primer. Bricks were sponged on with the initial wall glazes, and "cracks" were applied with feathers and thinned paint. The branches and leaves of the tree were stenciled in a freeform manner into the corner and along the ceiling line. Designed and stenciled by Susan Kolb.

A window casing, shutters, and a flower-filled window box culminate an impressive trompe l'oeil garden view. The wall was first painted with a satin-finish latex paint, then glazed with three washes consisting of white satin latex paint mixed with universal tints thinned with Floetrol (a paint additive) and water. Working from dark to light, the washes were applied with a large natural sponge. After the background view was sponged in, the window stencil, which required fifteen overlays, was stenciled with acrylics and large (at least ⅝ inch) stencil brushes. The image was then refined with a smaller brush. Trompe l'oeil window by Jan Dressler.

# CREATING A FANTASY

The concept of the trompe l'oeil fantasy room takes the idea of the "stenciled environment" (see pages 64–67) a few steps further. Although the scale of a trompe l'oeil project might be comparable to a stenciled one, trompe l'oeil's visual detail offers a wider range of creative possibilities, from the purely decorative (adorning a room) to the thoroughly practical (solving problems of light, color, and space). Although the examples shown below and on pages 120 and 121 primarily illustrate the former, each was designed to at least complement, if not enhance, the space in which it is located.

*Trompe l'oeil stenciling in several guises was used to transform a third-floor landing and hallway into a splendid garden terrace. To make the stencil for the wrought iron gate, a photograph of an antique iron gate was made into a slide and projected on the wall. The projected image was then traced and the stencils cut from the life-size drawing. Designed and stenciled by Ginny Eilertson.*

A medieval castle is the theme of this marvelously detailed decor, which features a real suit of armor. The walls were first basecoated with white latex paint, then randomly rolled along their bottom half with a sand-colored latex paint to create the effect of stone. The castle was stenciled with several overlays, including one for the stone, one for the mortar, four for the shingled turret roof, and two for the hinges and door knockers on the closet doors. The large, open space of the castle's walls were filled in with a rolling technique. Heavy shading was added around the tops of the castle walls to create depth. A sea sponge was used to randomly sponge on the clouds. Designed and stenciled by Constance Dehnel and Mary C. Valentine.

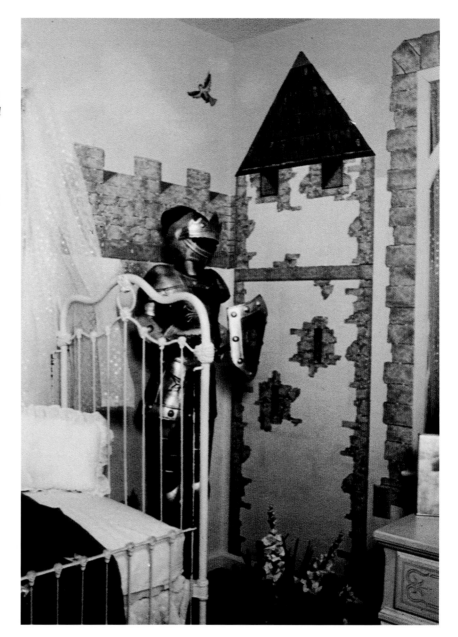

Textured drywall provided an excellent surface for this inspired southwestern decor. Red and gold chili peppers festoon an arched window, and a 7-foot-tall saguaro cactus displays a cowboy hat. The saguaro was placed in the corner of the room to accentuate the three-dimensional quality of its outstretched arms, which were created by reversing the same stencil. Both the boots and the lasso were produced with stencils, while the crate on which they are displayed was composed with masking tape. Painted antique furniture, Mexican pottery, and burlap pillows are but a few of the accessories used to perfect the atmosphere of this Mexican cantina. Stencils from L 'n J Designs; designed and stenciled by Linda Nelson Johnson and Lori Rohde; photo by Randy C. Rohde, Footprint Film, Inc.

This magnificent cumulus cloudscape adorns the ceiling and wall of a small spa bathroom. The ceiling and upper part of the wall were painted with sky blue, then the lower part was painted with shell pink. The colors were then blended at midpoint with a brush and a small amount of white paint. Irregularly shaped cloud stencils were used to establish the outline of the large cloud, and both stencils and cutouts were used to create the internal billows. The right side of the cloud was highlighted with white and stenciled with warm colors, while the left side was shaded and shadowed with several cool colors. Hard edges were softened with a piece of foam sponge. Some smaller clouds, including a few stratus wisps, were added to the background. (Right) Two cherubs confer near the edge of a cloud. Designed and stenciled by Peggy Decker.

# SPECIAL EFFECTS

In decorative painting, special effects run the gamut, from basic brush techniques like scumbling and blending, to color variations applied with glazes and washes, to the distinctive "faux" textures of sponging, rag- or bag-rolling, and marbling. When combined with stenciling, these techniques offer an infinite number of creative choices.

In the examples on these two pages, the decision to use a special effect was based on each room's specific decorative requirements. For a store specializing in reproductions of 18th-century furnishings, Renee McCooey and Nancy Kimball achieved the "primitive" style not only through their faithful adaptation of the motifs of the era, but with the use of a sanding and glazing technique that "antiques" both the stencil prints and the wall surface. Starting with the "blank slate" of a small powder room, Peggy Decker created a sumptuous New Orleans–style decor by

stenciling its walls and ceiling with faux rolled velvet featuring a fleur-de-lis print.

How do you select the appropriate technique for your project? Before you start, list the specific qualities of texture and pattern you hope to achieve, then consider the context in which the technique will be used. Details such as tools, consistency of paint, color mixing, and random or patterned application will be resolved as you experiment with and combine workable options.

As you experiment, keep in mind that, when used imprudently, a special effect can easily become too much of a good thing. Take the time to frankly assess whether an effect actually enhances a stencil design and contributes favorably to a decor, or if it simply calls attention to itself— an effect for effect's sake—which could compromise a project's integrity.

*The flat door of this powder room was given an elegant treatment with six recessed panels. The rolled velvet walls are faux-finish mastery achieved exclusively with stencils and paint. Designed and stenciled by Peggy Decker.*

Although the original itinerant stencilers were not concerned with the balanced distribution of elements in a full wall pattern, the designers felt that their precise placement would be more aesthetically pleasing. After the motifs were stenciled with acrylic paints (and very little shading), they were lightly sanded with fine sandpaper, leaving some areas essentially intact while wearing others away almost completely. Working with glazes requires certain safety precautions, including opening windows for maximum ventilation and wearing latex gloves to protect hands. After the ceiling and woodwork were taped, the glaze was applied by two people to accelerate the application process and to increase working time with the glaze. The first person dipped a large sea sponge into the glaze, blotted it on a paper towel, then dabbed it on the walls unevenly so that some areas remained unglazed. Working immediately behind, the second person picked up excess glaze and redeposited it onto unglazed areas by dabbing the wall with a large sea sponge dampened with water. (Left) The reaction between the glaze and the water created soft, mottled color and an oatmeal-like texture. For the corners, each wall was taped off and sponged individually, then a brush was used to apply glaze within the corner. Finally, additional glaze was applied with a smaller sponge to areas that would naturally discolor with age, such as corners and above the chair rail. Master Series Stencils from MB Historic Decor; designed and stenciled by Renee McCooey and Nancy Kimball.

*To help expand your client base and broaden the appeal of your work, take advantage of all your interests and skills. Designed and stenciled by Judith Barker.*

# STARTING YOUR OWN BUSINESS

Your stenciling experience is growing, and the quality and style of your work are helping to build your reputation as an artist and designer. You haven't bid a job professionally because all of your stenciling projects were done for family and friends. Eventually, however, the question arises: "What would you charge to stencil my dining room?" The moment of truth! You don't want to bid too high and risk losing the job, but you also don't want to bid so low that your time and talents aren't properly compensated for. How do you figure out what your work is worth? And once you've started your business, how do you find new clients?

# BECOMING A PROFESSIONAL STENCILER

Now that you're comfortable making important decisions about your own home decor and your work has sufficiently impressed someone to inquire about your creative services, you can use your painting, cutting, and planning skills as stepping stones to a career and business in stenciling.

## THE BIDDING PROCESS

These guidelines were developed out of trial and error—on jobs that were grossly under- and overbid—and are meant to provide fledgling professionals with a foundation on which to build a job estimate.

- *Don't bid a job over the phone.* Even though your customer thinks she knows the dimensions of the room and what she wants in it, you should always visit the site in person and measure a room before committing to a price.
- *Don't bid a job by the hour.* The statement, "I charge $X per hour" immediately invites the inevitable and often unanswerable question, "How many hours will it take?"
- *Don't begin a custom job without a firm price for a predetermined set of designs and colors.* If you submit a bid based on one set of conditions, and after you've begun your client constantly changes her mind, your original bid won't reflect the amount of time and effort you'll spend to complete the job. Your customer should understand that mid-course changes mean additional time *and* additional cost.

## SETTING A PRICING STRUCTURE

The following is a basic formula for developing a pricing structure for horizontal and vertical designs:

1. Determine precisely the amount of time required to measure and stencil 3 to 5 feet (or a single repeat) of each design in your portfolio, even if it means doing them over again from scratch. You can always use the additional proofs for presentations.
2. Determine a realistic hourly wage for your work. Approximately $15 to $20 per hour are reasonable rates for a beginning professional. Before you commit to a rate (or a job), investigate the rates of professional housepainters in your area. You shouldn't charge any less for your stenciling.
3. Price each design. For example, Design A can be measured and stenciled relatively quickly—5 feet in 10 minutes, or 30 feet per hour. At $15 per hour, the charge for Design A would be $0.50 per foot. In contrast, Design B is much more complex. With overlays and shading, you can only stencil 5 feet per hour. At $15 per hour, your charge for Design B would be $3 per foot.

   For central motifs or spot designs, determine a "per-pattern" price and multiply by the number of designs.

### OTHER CONSIDERATIONS

Always review the various factors that apply to each specific job before giving your client a price. Then present your client with a completely itemized bid on an estimate form.

When figuring your price per foot, you should also take into account:

- *Design.* Are you stenciling a finished design from your portfolio, or do you have to design an original stencil to coordinate with an established decor? Design time should be billed out at either an hourly fee or figured into your per-foot charge. For instance, in addition to charging $3 per foot to stencil a finished design, you would calculate and add to it an additional $1.50 per foot, or bill a separate flat fee for designing and cutting the stencils and preparing proofs.
- *Travel.* Is the job close to your home or studio, or do you have to travel 50 to 60 miles a day? Remember that time spent traveling and the wear and tear on your car is money, and you should charge for it.
- *Set-up and tear-down.* Can you leave your ladders and other equipment in place until the job is completed? If not, you should charge for the additional time spent setting up and tearing down your equipment.
- *Overhead.* Factor in your advertising, insurance, and fixed expenses into each job by adding an overhead percentage to each bid. For example, if the total per-foot estimated price for a room is $200, add another 10 to 20 percent for fixed expenses, making the total bid $220 to $240.

## ESTABLISHING A MINIMUM

Is it worth your time to accept a job whose estimated billings are below a certain dollar amount? Perhaps when you're first starting out, it's worth the exposure you'll receive, but once your business is established, is it still worth your time to accept such a job? Some professional stencilers establish minimums or base amounts, and won't do a job for less. Before you accept a job, you must calculate whether it's worth *all* the time you'll spend on it, whether designing, traveling, or stenciling.

The basic economic principle of supply and demand can easily come into play with your pricing structure. As your reputation escalates, you can be more selective about the jobs you take and demand a higher fee per job. Remember, if your prices are too low, you'll be very busy, but you won't be using your time to its best advantage. By being selective and developing a quality image, you can make more money without running yourself ragged.

## ADVICE FROM A PROFESSIONAL

Stephanie A. Crabb, an experienced professional stenciler, begins the bidding process by taking into account her preparation time and all her materials, in addition to estimating costs for time spent designing, stenciling, or traveling to and from the site.

In a project that involved stenciling a wine cellar, Stephanie first considered its surface preparation requirements. She noted the iron beam and post in the middle of the cellar, which would receive the majority of the stenciling, as well as the textured wall onto which the stenciling would continue. She then selected and purchased a precut stencil to harmonize with the purpose of the space—a border of grape leaves—which she intended to stencil with airbrush, adding vines by hand. Her bid included costs for the following:

- *Half the cost of the stencil.* Although Stephanie purchased the stencil for this particular job, the client should be expected to defray only half its cost, since she could add it to her stencil collection and use it again on another job.
- *Supplies.* If the client requests a look or technique that involves equipment or supplies that you don't normally use or have on hand, you should add their full costs to your estimate. For paints, paper proofs, and other miscellaneous supplies, charge a flat fee based on the size of the project.
- *Surface preparation.* The time required for this part of a stenciling project can easily exceed time spent stenciling, and should be carefully estimated.

After they reviewed the bid, the clients initialed it, as well as any changes they *both* agreed on. Stephanie requires a nonrefundable deposit equal to half the total estimated cost, with the remainder due at the completion of the job. She always documents her time and the colors, materials, and supplies she uses as reference for future bids.

Above all, be flexible in your estimating practices. Because it included several stencils, which could become quite complicated for the client and expensive for both parties, Stephanie bid her outdoor garden project (see page 101) with two different prices per foot, so that the clients could decide how full they wanted their garden to be. Stephanie's clients were then able to choose from an unlimited palette and selection of floral designs, with the understanding that they would receive a certain number of flowers and plants for a set amount of money. For instance, three to five designs per foot, as opposed to six to eight designs per foot, which would cost more.

## EXPANDING YOUR CLIENT BASE

Many new professionals can be heard to say, "Where I live, there's just no interest in all of this. I don't think I'll ever develop a customer base—the people here just don't know what stenciling is!" If you're at a loss as to how to create interest in stenciling—and specifically in your own work—take heart! There are no limits to the number of potential customers you can have. You just need to know how to stimulate them.

- *Promote stenciling's flexibility and accessibility.* Stenciling has become so much more than a craft. It's a way for people to make a home decorating statement and to put a bit of their personality into their homes, either by hiring a custom stenciler or by learning to stencil on their own. The real beauty of this decorating phenomenon is that the supplies are so easy to use. Even first-time stencilers can achieve great-looking results with no special painting skills when using a precut beginner border design. For this custom stenciler, to design a stylized motif to blend with an established decor presents an endless array of challenges and opportunities.

- *Know the trends.* An increasing number of home decor, craft, and women's magazines are featuring stenciling. The trend in custom stenciling is toward a more freeform style, a real departure from the rigid primitive motifs that were so popular in the 1970s and the early 1980s.

- *See and be seen.* If you're a professional stenciler, you must ensure that your work is seen by as many people as possible. Stencil a public space, such as the children's room in your local library or a doctor's waiting room. Contact your local newspaper. The editor of the home decorating or community pages might be interested in writing a story about your company. Wear stenciled clothing—or make some for your children to wear to school!

- *Learn to teach.* Conducting classes, workshops, and demonstrations can provide excellent opportunities to create interest in your stenciling. Contact schools (many public high schools offer adult or continuing education programs), churches, scouting troops, and senior citizens groups, or any group in your area that might be interested in sponsoring you. You'll be surprised at how eager some of these organizations are to sponsor special programs. Also, many retail craft and art supply stores schedule workshops and demonstrations. The most important thing to remember is that you're selling yourself as well as your stenciling, and that the people you're selling to are more interested in home decorating than in small craft projects.

- *Become a member.* Regardless of the kind of business you own or are involved in, you should take advantage of the opportunities offered by a professional organization. These often include networking, professional advice, up-to-date information, and education (including classes and certification programs). Professional stencilers can join the Stencil Artisans League, Inc. (SALI), which offers all of these services and currently has chapters in sixteen states and Canada. In addition to providing local support for professional stencilers through its local chapters, SALI also hosts a yearly convention and trade show. For information on membership or forming your own local chapter, contact SALI at their international headquarters: P.O. Box 920190, Norcross, Georgia, 30092; (770) 455-7258 (both phone and FAX).

Your market as a professional stenciler or a teacher is only as big as you think it is. Treat each person you meet as a potential customer or student, and your enthusiasm will become contagious! Set your sights high, and don't let petty excuses stymie the great potential within you or around you.

# WORKING WITH PATTERNS

This section contains stencil patterns for one practice cutting session and two projects. These patterns, which range from extremely simple to fairly complex, vary in the level of cutting and stenciling skill they require.

Since the patterns have been reduced to fit on the pages of this book, you'll need to enlarge them if you want to use them at full size. There are a few methods of enlarging and reducing patterns, including drawing a consistent grid over the original image, then redrawing the image within a proportionally larger or smaller grid. The easiest (and fastest) way is to use a photocopy machine that enlarges and reduces—just use the percentage for enlargement that accompanies each pattern.

A word of caution that bears repeating: While it is permissible to copy or adapt the design of a fabric, wallpaper, or other item for use in your own home, it is a violation of copyright law to trace a precut stencil pattern.

# PRACTICE DESIGN

Use at same size. Refer to page 22 for cutting instructions.

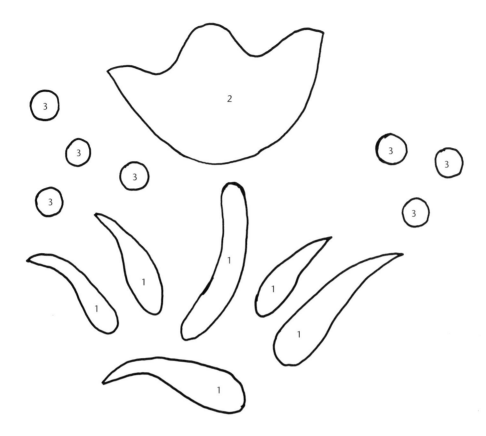

# SEA SHELL TILE DESIGNS

Use both patterns at same size. See pages 88–89 for a
demonstration by Carol Phippen. Designed by Susan Saye.

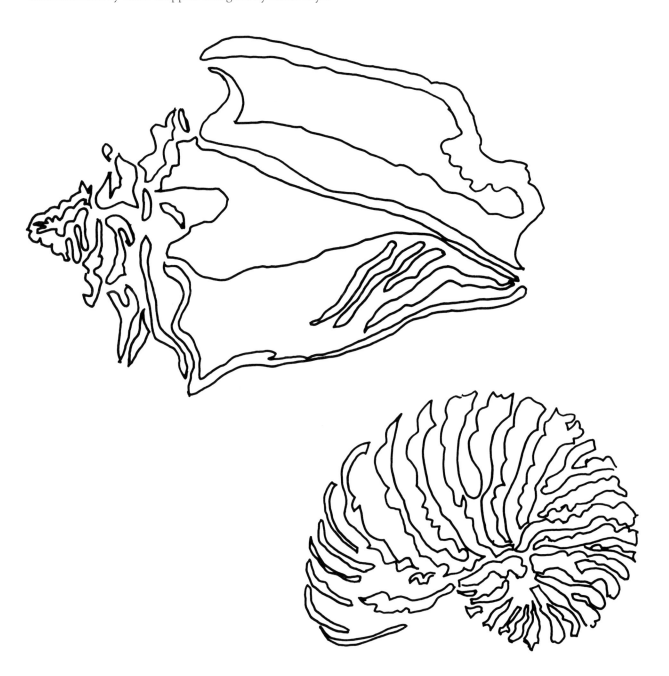

# IVY TILE RUG (COMPLETE PATTERN)

The complete pattern of the ivy tile rug on page 90 is shown below (enlarge 172%). Its three overlays—the leaves, the highlights and vines, and the ribbon—are on pages 132–134. The three overlays for the fringe are on page 135. Designed by Jane Gauss.

IVY TILE RUG: OVERLAY 1
(LEAVES AND REGISTRATION MARKS)
Enlarge 172%

132

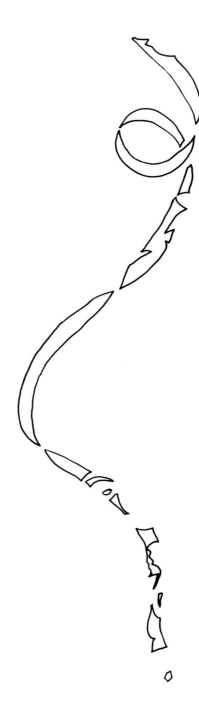

IVY TILE RUG FRINGE:
OVERLAYS 1 THROUGH 3
Enlarge 114%

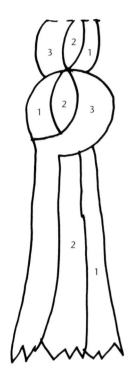

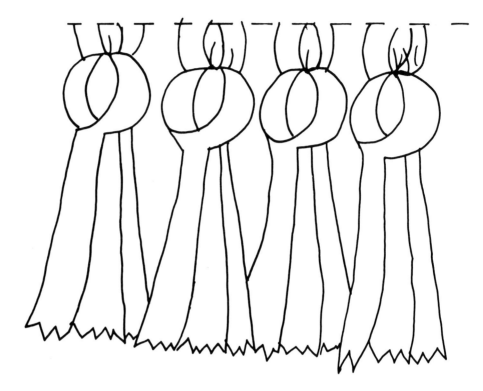

Separate into overlays as indicated.

Use this pattern to create a continuous fringe. Use the single-tassel pattern at left as a guide to cutting overlays.

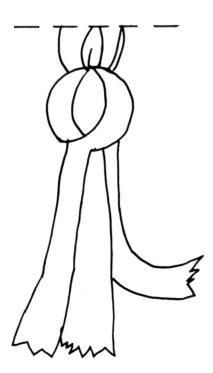

Add a tossed tassel randomly within the fringe.
Flop the stencil for a reversed tossed tassel.

# CONTRIBUTORS

All of the stencilers whose work appears in this book are members of the Stencil Artisans League, Inc. (SALI), an international organization comprised of professional and amateur stencilers, faux finishers, and other decorative painters. In addition to sponsoring an annual convention at which members can participate in a variety of workshops and seminars, SALI conducts a two-tier certification program that recognizes members' outstanding work. The designations, which are noted beside each certified stenciler's name in the list below, are as follows:

CS       Certified Stenciler
CMS    Certified Master Stenciler
CST     Certified Stenciling Teacher
CMST   Certified Master Stenciler Teacher

For information on membership, certification, and other services, call or write
Stencil Artisans League, Inc.
P.O. Box 920190
Norcross, Georgia 30092
(770) 455-7258 (phone and FAX)

Accompanying the contact information for each designer are the page or pages on which their work appears.

**Anita Alsup**
The Finishing Touch
12118 Cedar Circle
Sainte Genevieve, Missouri 63670
(314) 483-3211
*pages 11 and 93*

**Lu Ann Anderson**
ILB Designs - Illusions by Lu
231 Sheboygan Street
Fond du Lac, Wisconsin 54935
(414) 922-9015
*page 80*

**Marjorie Andreae**
Andreae Designs
5232 South Locustwood Drive
Fort Gratiot, Michigan 48059
(810) 385-4631
*page 67*

**Judith Barker, CS-CST**
American Traditional
Route 4, Box 317A
Northwood, New Hampshire 03261
(603) 942-8100
FAX: (603) 942-8919
*pages 1, 32, 83, 94, 97–98, and 124–125*

**Adele Bishop**
Adele Bishop, Inc.
P.O. Box 3349
Kinston, North Carolina 28501
(919) 527-4186
*pages 11, 14–15, 44–45, 76, 79, and 117*

**Sandra and Linda Buckingham**
Buckingham Stencils, Inc.
Suite 1107-1574 Gulf Road
Point Roberts, Washington 98281
(604) 943-2029
FAX: (604) 943-3143
*pages 28–29, 37, 38, 63, 65, and 116*

**Julia Hierl Burmesch, CS**
Finishing Touch Stencils
732 Birch Lane
Northfield, Minnesota 55057
(507) 663-6059
*pages 1, 38, 57, 83, and 96*

**Stephanie A. Crabb**
Custom Stenciling
25883 South Carmel Hills Drive
Carmel, California 93923
(408) 626-5459
*pages 102 and 126–127*

**Jo Bach Crary**
P.O. Box 697
Boothbay Harbor, Maine 04538
(207) 633-3385
*page 114*

**Vi and Stu Cutbill**
Cutbill & Company
2006-75 Queen Street North
Hamilton, Ontario, Canada L8R 3J3
(905) 547-8525
FAX: (905) 547-8191
*pages 12, 56, and 94*

**Peggy Decker, CMS-CMST**
Makin-It-Peggy Decker Stencils
1604 Beaver Creek Lane
Snellville, Georgia 30278
(404) 985-1382
*pages 121 and 122*

**Constance Dehnel**
Custom Stenciling by Constance
12837 Valleywood Drive
Woodbridge, Virginia 22192
(703) 494-3235
*page 120*

**Bunny DeLorie and Kathy Curtis**
FeFiFaux Finish
1052 Vereda Del Ciervo
Goleta, California 93117
(805) 968-1905
*page 55*

**Jan Demerath**
Wall Stenciling by Jan
31242 Comotilo Court
Temecula, California 92592
(909) 676-1768
*pages 23 and 55*

**Jan Dressler, CS**
The Itinerant Stenciler
11030 173rd Avenue S.E.
Renton, Washington 98059
(206) 226-0306
FAX: (206) 226-9556
*pages 54, 61, 75, 107, and 118*

**Linda Durkin, CS**
3303 Goodley Road
Boothwyn, Pennsylvania 19061
(610) 497-0310
*page 69*

**Ginny Eilertson, CS**
Stenciling Etc.
35 Noon Hill Avenue
Norfolk, Massachusetts 02056
(508) 528-0378
*page 119*

**Peggy Eisenberg**
Decorative Accents
111 Comstock Road
Woodside, California 94062
(415) 851-7110
*pages 56 and 76*

**Pat Fielder**
Boxwood Designs
630 Gladstone S.E.
East Grand Rapids, Michigan 49506
(616) 452-4508
*pages 91 and 92*

**Patricia Flournoy**
Ambiente, Inc.
410 East 57th Street
New York, New York 10022
(212) 980-0151
*page 87*

**Polly Forcier**
MB Historic Decor
P.O. Box 880
Norwich, Vermont 05055
(802) 649-1790
FAX: (802) 649-1791
*pages 8 and 123*

**Jane Gauss**
Stenciler's Emporium, Inc.
9261 Ravenna Road - Unit B-3-34
Twinsburg, Ohio 44087
(216) 425-1766
FAX: (216) 963-7844
*pages 2–3, 11, 13, 47, 79, 90, and 131–135*

**Sherry Gholson**
Brush Strokes Custom Painting
RR 4, #91
Carmi, Illinois 62821
(618) 382-4730
*pages 60–61*

**Christina Gibson**
Elegant Whimsey
3008 Seminole Road
Woodbridge, Virginia 22192
(703) 491-3889
*pages 64 and 74*

**Toni Grove, CS**
8962 Columbia Road
Olmsted Falls, Ohio 44138
(216) 235-5252
*page 58*

**Jean Hansen**
Jean Hansen Publications
308 Pettipaug Road
Westbrook, Connecticut 06498
(203) 399-9516
FAX: (203) 399-4276
*pages 108 and 109*

**Sheri Hoeger**
The Mad Stencilist
2529 Pendleton Drive
El Dorado Hills, California 95762
(916) 933-1790
*pages 63, 68, 80, 96, 107, and 111*

**Ann Hooe**
Ann Hooe Ltd.
P.O. Box 9
Winnetka, Illinois 60093
(708) 446-7749
FAX: (708) 446-7769
*pages 55 and 56*

**Elizabeth Hurbis**
Painted Endeavors
19215 Riverside Drive
Birmingham, Michigan 48025
(313) 646-7668
*page 99*

**Barbara N. Johnson**
P.O. Box 2112
Marco Island, Florida 33969
(813) 642-7641
*page 87*

**Dawne Marie Johnson**
Dawne Marie Designs
32500 Lofton Avenue
Chisago City, Minnesota 55013
(612) 257-2741
*pages 54 and 75*

**Linda Nelson Johnson**
L 'n J Designs
110 West University Drive
Mesa, Arizona 85201
(602) 833-4565
*pages 13, 69, and 121*

**Martha Johnson, CS**
7369 Ridge Road
Lockport, New York 14094
(716) 772-7280
*pages 52–53*

**Dee Keller**
DeeSigns Ltd.
P.O. Box 960
Newnan, Georgia 30264
(404) 304-1993
*pages 76, 87, 101, and 112*

**Nancy Kimball, CS-CST**
McKim & Company
10 Ridgefield Drive
East Greenwich, Rhode Island 02818
(401) 884-4607 (phone andFAX)
*page 123*

**Susan Kolb**
Studio Designs by Susan
922 Kilbourn Avenue
West Bend, Wisconsin 53095
(414) 334-1498
*pages 13 and 118*

**Linda Carter Lefko**
1277 Elmira Road
Penn Yan, New York 14527
(315) 536-4248
*pages 10, 68, and 123*

**Carol Lumpkin**
Decorative Artist
3189 Chamblee-Tucker Road
Atlanta, Georgia 30341
(404) 458-5990
*pages 42–43*

**Renee McCooey**
McKim & Company
21 Tucker Hollow Road
North Scituate, Rhode Island 02857
(401) 647-5636
*page 123*

**Jeanette McKibben, CS**
McKibben & Company
P.O. Box 470
Hampton, Florida 32044
(904) 485-1747
FAX: (904) 468-1846
*page 58*

**Mary Jane Malinoski, CS**
16 Winter Court
Effort, Pennsylvania 18330
(717) 620-0946
FAX: (717) 620-4350
*page 117*

**Carol Martell**
13401 Chestnut Oak Drive
Gaithersburg, Maryland 20878
(301) 840-9488
*page 87*

**Jo Miller**
44355 Cadburry
Clinton Township, Michigan 48038
(810) 263-1197
*pages 58, 63, and 100*

**Lee Anne Miller**
6827 Van Hyning Road
Deansboro, New York 13328
(315) 821-6113
*pages 86 and 103*

**Deb Mores**
Deb Mores Designs, Inc.
5 Mount Rascal Road
Hackettstown, New Jersey 07840
(908) 813-8855
*pages 33, 35, and 61*

**Carol Phippen**
103 Jefferson Circle
Atlanta, Georgia 30328
(404) 396-8749
*pages 88–89*

**Linda Radziminski, CS-CST**
359 White Road
Mineola, New York 11501
(516) 294-0525
*pages 99, 112, and 117*

**Sharon Ranney**
1012 Galloping Hill Road
Fairfield, Connecticut 06430
(203) 255-9702
*page 117*

**Diane Patricia Rich**
Golden Artist Colors, Inc.
Bell Road
New Berlin, New York 13411
(607) 847-6154
FAX: (607) 847-6767
*page 85*

**Julie Robinson**
35673 Ashford Drive
Sterling Heights, Michigan 48312
(313) 826-3404
*page 67*

**Linda M. Rogers, CS**
RR 1, Box 524-B
Heyworth, Illinois 61745
(309) 473-2740
*page 74*

**Lori Rohde**
1676 South Villas Lane
Chandler, Arizona 85248
(602) 963-0380
*pages 69 and 121*

**Melanie Royals, CS**
Royal Design Studio
1854 Ithaca Street
Chula Vista, California 91913
(619) 421-4507
*pages 33, 38, 59, and 100*

**Vladimir and Olga Rozenshtein**
Stencillusions by V & Olga
159 Beach 123rd Street
Rockaway Park, New York 11694
(718) 318-0081
FAX: (718) 634-4415
*page 115*

**Anne Rullman, CS**
Stenciling Associates
12525 Colony Road
Dunlap, Illinois 61525
(309) 243-9621
*pages 62, 73, and 101*

**Susan Saye**
Saye Tiles
3459 Havalyn Lane
Doraville, Georgia 30340
(770) 457-5195
FAX: (770) 455-7258
*pages 88–89, 90, and 130*

**Mary Severns, CS**
9032 Deerslayer Road
Parker, Colorado 80134
(303) 841-7605
*pages 54 and 57*

**Chris Smith**
Stencils 'n Stuff
119 Elm Street
East Bridgewater, Massachusetts
02333
(508) 378-4587
*page 58*

**Eileen Snell, CS**
Sensations
3999 Winters Hill Drive
Atlanta, Georgia 30360
(404) 393-8127
*page 114*

**Maureen Soens, CS**
Maureen's Decorative Paint Finishes
831 Augusta Drive
Rochester Hills, Michigan 48309
(810) 651-6846
*page 92*

**Laurie Spagnolia**
10 Elm Street
Madison, New Jersey 07940
(201) 765-0202
*page 102*

**Catherine A. Stone**
272 South West Street
Carlisle, Pennsylvania 17013
(717) 243-4060
*page 66*

**Marie Sturmer, CS-CST**
8827 Sunset Circle
Traverse City, Michigan 49684
(616) 941-2849
*page 82*

**Lynn Terrel**
Stenciling Associates
107 Wildflower Way
Dunlap, Illinois 61525
(309) 243-9292
*pages 62, 73, and 101*

**P. J. Tetreault**
43 Lockrow Boulevard
Albany, New York 12205
(518) 438-8020 (phone and FAX)
*pages 69, 77, 83, 103, 109, 110, 112, 113, and 115*

**Nancy Tribolet**
Stencil Designs by Nancy
15206 Walters Road
Houston, Texas 77068
(713) 893-6187
*pages 36, 74, 87, and 117*

**Mary C. Valentine**
P.O. Box 426
Potsdam, New York 13676
(315) 265-3593
*page 120*

**Heather Whitehouse**
Artistic Surfaces
165 Colchester Avenue
East Hampton, Connecticut 06424
(203) 267-0715
*pages 57 and 116*

**Caroline Ann Zarrilli**
2306 Bryn Mawr Avenue
Ardmore, Pennsylvania 19003
(215) 649-0340
*pages 81 and 95*

# RETAILERS, WHOLESALERS, AND MANUFACTURERS

The following is a listing of sources for a range of stenciling supplies, including stencils, paints, mediums, and applicators. Wherever applicable, the pages on which a company's products are referred to accompany the listing.

Your best sources for stenciling supplies are your local craft and art supply stores, where knowledgeable staff can advise you on your purchases. If you need something they don't have in stock, they can usually order it for you. If you can't locate a retail source for stenciling supplies in your area, you can try contacting one of the retailers listed below. In addition to accepting phone and mail order sales from individual customers, some sell their own product lines at a discount to other retailers. In contrast, wholesalers and manufacturers sell only to retailers, but will gladly direct you to the retailer nearest you that carries their products and provide you with technical assistance. If you've exhausted all these avenues and still can't find a product, or if you need more information, call the Stencil Artisans League, Inc. (SALI) at (770) 445-7258 (phone and FAX).

## RETAILERS

### ALABAMA
**THAT'S A STENCIL?**
CORINNE HINDS
2029 VALLEYDALE ROAD
BIRMINGHAM, ALABAMA 35244
(205) 987-1522

### CALIFORNIA
**Country Painting**
Gina Leonard
910 North California Street
Burbank, California 91505
(818) 841-4559

**Elegant Designs**
Trudy Dewyer Collins
2863 West Athens Avenue
Fresno, California 93711
(209) 438-8282

**Holly Hocks & Co.**
Carmen Takemoto
c/o 10871 North Wolfe Road
Cupertino, California 95014
(408) 255-3546
FAX: (408) 777-9653

**KJs Craft Barn**
Karen Matz
27 West 10th Street
Tracy, California 95376
(209) 835-4850

**Mic Depot 39, Inc.**
Lulu Mota
1866 West 169th Street - Suite D
Gardena, California 90247
(310) 516-6635

**Paint Magic**
Patricia Orlando
2426 Fillmore Street
San Francisco, California 94115
(415) 292-7780
FAX: (415) 292-7782

**Royal Design Studio**
Melanie Royals, CS
1854 Ithaca Street
Chula Vista, California 91913
(619) 421-4507

**The Cottage Faire**
Carol Wilson
6930 Village Parkway
Dublin, California 94508
(510) 447-8936

**The Cube Store Unfinished Wood Furniture**
Scott Harring
1305 Tennessee Street
Valejo, California 94590
(707) 649-2823
FAX: (707) 644-9112

**The Mad Stencilist**
Sheri Hoeger
2529 Pendleton Drive
El Dorado Hills, California 95762
(916) 933-1790

**The Stencil House**
Mary Johnson
610-A Main Street
Pleasanton, California 94566
(510) 846-0950

**The Stencilled Garden**
Jennifer Ferguson
1764 West Bullard
Fresno, California 93711
(209) 277-9460

**Wooden Spool**
Claudia Horn
P.O. Box 538
Elk Grove, California 95759
(916) 685-1315

### CONNECTICUT
**Creative Craft Center**
Selina McArdle
96 Elm Street
Cheshire, Connecticut 06410
(203) 272-5897
FAX: (203) 272-1991

**Jean Hansen Publications**
Jean Hansen
308 Pettipaug Road
Westbrook, Connecticut 06498
(203) 399-9516
FAX: (203) 399-4276

**The Village Tole Shop Nutmeg Stencilers**
Shirley Day
1286 Mountain Road
West Suffield, Connecticut 06093
(203) 668-2703

### DELAWARE
**Stenciled Interiors**
Marge Stitz
144 Lantana Square
Hockessin, Delaware 19707
(302) 234-2024

### FLORIDA
**The Stencil Collection**
Deborah Chychota
22260 Sag Harbor Court - #2
Wellington, Florida 33414
(404) 798-0570

### GEORGIA
**DeeSigns Ltd.**
Gene Keller
P.O. Box 960
Newnan, Georgia 30264
(404) 304-1993

**Makin-It-Peggy Decker Stencils**
Peggy Decker, CMS-CMST
1604 Beaver Creek Lane
Snellville, Georgia 30276
(404) 985-1382

ILLINOIS
**Ann Hooe Ltd.**
Ann Hooe
P.O. Box 9
Winnetka, Illinois 60093
(708) 446-7749
FAX: (708) 446-7769

**Designer Home Stencils**
Lenore Babka
1618 West Algonquin Road
Hoffman Estates, Illinois 60195
(708) 991-8930
FAX: (708) 991-1677

**Jay Lee Home & Crafts**
Arlene Bransky
395C Cary Algonquin Road
Cary, Illinois 60013
(708) 540-0171

**L & S Stencil Studio**
Patricia Seliga
36 South Washington - Suite 1
Hinsdale, Illinois 60521
(708) 654-8977

**Ms. Elaineous Business**
Elaine Hemker
1308 Plum Avenue
Mount Vernon, Illinois 62864
(618) 234-3986

**Saxton Home Decor**
Beverly Saxton
227 West Maple
New Lenox, Illinois 60451
(815) 485-4101

**Stencil Home Gallery**
Sandra Barker
205 West Gold Road
Schaumburg, Illinois 60194
(708) 882-7373
also
654 South Route 59
Naperville, Illinois 60540
(708) 357-4300

**The Picket Fence**
Peggy Kepp
901 Broadway
Mattoon, Illinois 61938
(217) 235-3936

**The Stencil Stop**
Barbara Pedraza
7816 Bennington Court
Woostock, Illinois 60098
(815) 363-1450

**The Stencil Studio**
Honey Schaeffer
303 Franklin Street
Geneva, Illinois 60134
(708) 208-5051

INDIANA
**The Painter's Daughter**
Elaine Lindemann
11829 Sand Dollar Court
Indianapolis, Indiana 46256
(317) 577-1457

KANSAS
**Penny's Designs Unlimited**
Penny Tyler
317 West Greeley
P.O. Box 622
Tribune, Kansas 67879
(316) 376-4948

MAINE
**Periwinkle Decorative Artists**
Janet Perry
36 Main Street
Kennebunk, Maine 04043
(207) 985-7046
*page 117*

MASSACHUSETTS
**Colonial Crafts**
Suzanne Phifer
Route 20 - Box 345
Sturbridge, Massachusetts 01566
(413) 347-3061
FAX: (508) 347-3061

**The Bittersweet Gallery**
William Beguerie
197 Rockland Street - Route 139
Hanover, Massachusetts 02339
(617) 826-3398

**The Stencil Shoppe of Plymouth, Massachusetts**
Kimberly Silva
16 Court Street
Plymouth, Massachusetts 02360
(508) 830-1163

MICHIGAN
**Andreae Designs**
Marjorie Andreae
5232 South Locustwood Drive
Fort Gratiot, Michigan 48059
(810) 385-4631

**Anne's Crafts**
Adrienne Smith
110 North Center
Northville, Michigan 48167
(810) 348-6810

**Stencils n' More**
Marcy McConnell, CS
22070 Goddard Road
Taylor, Michigan 48180
(313) 291-1575

MINNESOTA
**Sugar Creek Gallery**
Carol Olson
500 Pine Street
Chaska, Minnesota 55318
(612) 368-4669

**The Stamp Cottage**
Margaret Craven
115 West Main Street
Crosby, Minnesota 56441
(218) 678-3033 (phone and FAX)

MISSOURI
**Salt River Stencils**
Chris Groff
311 Main Street
St. Peters, Missouri 63376
(314) 397-6189

**Stenciling Center**
Ardis Preuss
132 West Monroe
Kirkwood, Missouri 63122
(314) 677-2151

NORTH CAROLINA
**Adele Bishop, Inc.**
R.T. Paul
P.O. Box 3349
Kinston, North Carolina 28501
(919) 527-4186

**Artifects**
Susan Warlick
325 Blake Street
Raleigh, North Carolina 27601
(919) 829-9288

**Not Just Stencils**
Lauren De Vido
203 Scotch Road
Ewing, New Jersey 08628
(609) 883-3702

**The Stencil Studio**
Amanda De Young
148 Main Street - Grist Mill Square
Pittstown, New Jersey 08867
(908) 730-9114

**Daniels Paint & Decorating Center**
Nancy Scherer
242 Main Street
Binghamton, New York 13905
(607) 798-0700

**It's Creative**
Patricia Bauscher
366 Route 910
Upper Nyack, New York 10960
(201) 767-0096

**Jan's Woodcroft**
Jan Dwyer
106 North Main Street
Fairport, New York 14450
(716) 377-3144

**Paint Decor Stencil Company**
Teresa Loesch
25-22 47th Street
Astoria, New York 11103
(718) 728-5012

**Patch As Patch Can**
Pam Aulson
85 Highland Road
Glen Cove, New York 11542
(516) 671-7342

**The Stencil Barn**
Roberta Brewster
RFD #1 - Box 29A
Saranac Lake, New York 12963
(518) 891-0176

**Stencillusions by V & Olga**
Vladimir Rozenshtein
159 Beach 123rd Street
Rockaway Park, New York 11694
(718) 318-0081
FAX: (718) 634-4415

**Woodpecker Crafts**
Betty Peck
RR #3 - Box 138 - Queens Highway
Kerhonkson, New York 12446
(914) 626-3575

**Pro Faux Workshop & Tool Company**
John Catalanotto
1367 Girard Street
Akron, Ohio 44301
(216) 773-4763
FAX: (216) 773-1983

**Stenciler's Emporium, Inc.**
Jane Gauss
9261 Ravenna Road - Unit B-3-B4
Twinsburg, Ohio 44087
(216) 425-1766
FAX: (216) 963-7844
Toll free in the U.S.: (800) 229-1760;
in Canada: (800) 339-7805

**Brickends Artisan Shop**
Gloria Keating
P.O. Box 389
Shawnee On Delaware, Pennsylvania 18356
(717) 476-4120

**Epoch Designs**
Kimberly Black
P.O. Box 4033
Elwyn, Pennsylvania 19053
(610) 525-7708

**Hatboro Stencil Shop**
Wallis & Bissie Miller
220 South York Road
Hatboro, Pennsylvania 19040
(215) 887-3222

**Historic Directions, Inc.**
317 East Main Street
Lock Haven, Pennsylvania 17745
(717) 748-6220

**Signature Stencils**
Patty Firsching
1847 Markley Street
Norristown, Pennsylvania 19401
(215) 279-3877

**Stencil Werks**
Carolyn Blahosky
1723 Tilghman Street
Allentown, Pennsylvania 18104
(610) 433-7776

**The Corner on Paint**
Esther Mager
P.O. Box 800
Brodheadsville, Pennsylvania 18322
(717) 992-2888

**The Stencil Kase**
Karen Christ
19 Morningside Drive
Lansdale, Pennsylvania 19446
(215) 362-6913

**The Stencil Shoppe, Inc.**
Helen Walker
39 Olde Ridge Village
Chadds Ford, Pennsylvania 19317
(215) 459-8362
FAX: (302) 477-0170

**The Stenciler**
Betty Russo
3646 Pottsville Pike
Reading, Pennsylvania 19605
(610) 921-9502

**Yowler & Shepps Stencils**
Lori Shepps
3529 Main Street
Conestoga, Pennsylvania 17516
(717) 872-2820

**Carolyn's Crafts**
Carolyn Morrissey
54 Phillips Street
Wickford, Rhode Island 02852
(401) 294-9359

**A Painted Treasure**
Pat Costantini
2001 Coit Road - #140
Plano, Texas 75075
(214) 985-4797
FAX: (214) 867-4275

**Michaels Stores, Inc.**
Brenda Lugannani
5931 Campus Circle Drive
Irving, Texas 75053
(214) 714-7153
FAX: (214) 714-7154

**The Village Wood Shoppe, Inc.**
Mary Shackleton
1095 West 7800 South - #12
West Jordan, Utah 84084
(801) 566-5227

**Decorative Arts Studio**
Kathie Marron-Wall
Route 30 - RR #1 - Box 136
Dorset, Vermont 05251
(802) 867-5955
*page 35*

**MB Historic Decor**
Polly Forcier
P.O. Box 880
Norwich, Vermont 05055
(802) 649-1790
FAX: (802) 649-1791

**Ewe & Me Pattern
Company/Craftlink**
Karen Booy
#586 - 200 West 3rd Street
Box 8000
Sumas, Washington 98295
(604) 820-8424

**Jan Dressler Stencils**
Jan Dressler, CS
11030 173rd Avenue S.E.
Renton, Washington 98059
(206) 226-0306
FAX: (206) 226-9556

**Stencil Delight**
Vickie Lyall
8919 Gravelly Lake Drive S.W.
Tacoma, Washington 98499
(206) 584-7623

**American Home Stencils, Inc.**
Ann Kooping
10007 South 76st Street
Franklin, Wisconsin 53132
(414) 425-5381
FAX: (414) 425-5381
*page 33*

**Craft Nook**
Jayne Addison
202 East Main Street
Sun Prairie, Wisconsin 53590
(608) 837-4699

**Jaclyn M. Art Gallery**
Judy Schroeder
P.O. Box 47
Antigo, Wisconsin 54409
(715) 623-4150

**Stamp n' Hand**
Margie Wanek
200 South 4th Street
La Crosse, Wisconsin 54601
(608) 784-1234

**Stencil Home Gallery**
Sandra Barker
2300 Pilgrim Road
Brookfield, Wisconsin 53005
(414) 797-9979

**The Painted Room**
Kathleen Zimmerman
1699 Schofield Avenue - #114
Schofield, Wisconsin 54476
(715) 359-0080

**Upstairs/Downstairs**
Joan Hulkick
537 Vernal Avenue
Milton, Wisconsin 53563
(414) 473-6570

**Willow Creek**
Debbie Harmon
P.O. Box 326
Osseo, Wisconsin 54758
(715) 597-2514

**Cutbill & Company**
Vi Cutbill
#2006-75 Queen Street North
Hamilton, Ontario L8R 3J3
(905) 547-8525

**Kindred Spirit Endeavors, Inc.**
Marie Browning
541½ Fisgard Street
Victoria, British Columbia V8W 1R3
(604) 385-4567

**Curio Cité**
Diane Chiasson
33 Isabella Street - Suite 105
Toronto, Ontario M4Y 2P7
(416) 926-1338
FAX: (416) 921-6994

**PCU Coatings Limited**
Jim Theobalds
502 Adelaide Street West
Toronto, Ontario M5V 1T2
(416) 366-0248
FAX: (416) 336-4538

## WHOLESALERS

**American Traditional Stencils**
Judy Barker, CS-CST
Route 4 - Box 317A
Northwood, New Hampshire 03261
(603) 942-8100
FAX: (603) 942-8919

## MANUFACTURERS

**DecoArt**
Etta Brown
Box 360
Stanford, Kentucky 40484
(606) 365-3193
FAX: (606) 365-9739

**Delta Technical Coatings**
Debbie Garner
2550 Pellisier Place
Whittier, California 90501
(800) 423-4135

**Golden Artist Colors, Inc.**
Diane Patricia Rich
Bell Road
New Berlin, New York 13411
(607) 847-6154
FAX: (607) 847-6767

**Laserworks**
Jeff Franklin
800 Church Street
Ripon, Wisconsin 54971
(414) 294-6544
FAX: (414) 294-6588

**N. E. Scale Models, Inc.**
Mr. Jean Oriol
99 Cross Street - P.O. Box 727
Methuen, Massachusetts 01844
(508) 688-6019
FAX: (508) 794-9104

**Robert Simmons Brushes**
A Division of Daler-Rowney USA
2 Corporate Drive
Cranbury, New Jersey 08512
(212) 675-3136
FAX: (212) 633-9237

**Stencil Decor**
A Division of Plaid Enterprises, Inc.
P.O. Box 7600
Norcross, Georgia 30091
*pages 41, 50, 75, and 80 (Mod-Podge)*

**Stencil Ease, Inc.**
P.O. Box 1127
Old Saybrook, Connecticut 06475
(203) 395-0150

**The Flood Company**
P.O. Box 2535
Hudson, Ohio 44236
(216) 650-4070
Technical support: (800) 321-3444
*pages 74 and 118 (manufacturers of Floetrol)*

**WM Zinsser & Co., Inc.**
Diane Wood
173 Belmont Drive
Somerset, New Jersey 08875
(908) 469-8100
FAX: (908) 563-9774

**XIM Products, Inc.**
Richard Hardy
1169 Bassett Road
Westlake, Ohio 44145
(216) 871-4737
FAX: (216) 871-3027
*pages 92 and 103*

# INDEX